THE OLD LADY
SAYS "NO!"

IRISH DRAMATIC TEXTS

THE OLD LADY
SAYS "NO!"

by Denis Johnston

Edited
with an Introduction and Notes
by Christine St. Peter

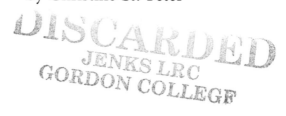
The Catholic University of America Press
Washington, D.C.

Colin Smythe
Gerrards Cross, Bucks.

Text of The Old Lady Says "No!" copyright © 1929
Denis Johnston
Introduction and other editorial matter
Copyright © 1992
The Catholic University of America Press

Printed in the United States of America
The paper used in this publication meets the minimum
requirements of American National Standards for
Information Science — Permanence of Paper for Printed
Library materials, ANSI Z39.48-1984.
∞

LIBRARY OF CONGRESS CATALOGING-IN-PUBLICATION DATA
Johnston, Denis, 1901 – 1984
    The old lady says "No!" / by Denis Johnston ;
edited, with an introduction and notes, by Christine
St. Peter.
        p.   cm. — (Irish dramatic texts)
    Includes bibliographical references.
    I. St. Peter, Christine.   II. Title.   III. Series.
PR6019.O397044   1992
822'.912 — dc20
91-22324
ISBN 0-8132-0751-7 (alk. paper)

BRITISH LIBRARY CATALOGING-IN-PUBLICATION DATA
A catalog record for this book is available from the
British Library.
ISBN 0-86140-357-6

CONTENTS

ACKNOWLEDGMENTS

I am grateful to the many people who have shared knowledge and resources, including Veronica O'Reilly, Felicity O'Mahoney, Stuart O Seanóir, Joseph Ronsley, Chris Petter, Nicholas Grene, F. J. E. Hurst, Margaret Vowles, John Tucker, Robert Mahony, and, most particularly, Ann Saddlemyer.

My acknowledgments to the following for permission to use manuscript materials: Michael Johnston for the Estate of Denis Johnston; Michael Yeats and John Kelly for Oxford University Press; the Library of Trinity College, Dublin; the Library of the New University of Ulster at Coleraine; the National Library of Ireland; the University of Victoria Special Collections; the Henry W. and Albert Berg Collection of the New York Public Library.

Finally, I wish to acknowledge the generous financial support of the Social Science and Humanities Research Council of Canada.

CHRONOLOGY

1901   William Denis Johnston born 18 June in Dublin, only child of William John Johnston and Kathleen Johnston, née King.

1908–15 Attends St. Andrew's College, Dublin.

1915–16 Attends Merchiston Castle School, Edinburgh.

1917–18 Attends St. Andrew's College, Dublin.

1919–23 Reads history and law at Christ's College, Cambridge.

1923–24 Completes LL.B. degree at Harvard Law School with dissertation, *The Implementation of the Anglo-Irish Treaty*.

1924   Works as seaman on S.M. Spaulding between Florida and Mexico.
      Joins Trinity Dramatics and Dublin Drama League.

1925   Called to English Bar (Inner Temple) and Irish Bar (King's Inn).
      Writes first play, *Continuous Performance,* later destroyed by author.

1926   Called to Northern Irish Bar.

1926   Begins practicing law in Dublin; continued this until 1936.
      Completes first version of *The Old Lady Says "No!"* (*Shadowdance*).

1927   Directs New Players in Georg Kaiser's *From Morn till Midnight,* first play staged in new Peacock Theatre.

1928   Marries Abbey actress Shelagh Richards in Dublin; two children by first marriage: daughter, writer Jennifer Johnston, and son, Michael.

Directs F. J. McCormick in *King Lear,* Abbey Theatre's first Shakespeare production.

Directs Eugene O'Neill's *The Fountain* and Ernst Toller's *Masses and Man* for Dublin Drama League.

1929   Directs Ernst Toller's *Hopplà* for Dublin Drama League.

Opening on 3 July of *The Old Lady Says "No!"* at Peacock Theatre, produced by newly formed Dublin Gate Theatre.

1931   Writes and directs ballet "La Chèvre indiscrète" for the *Dublin Review* of the Dublin Gate Theatre.

The Moon in the Yellow River produced at Abbey Theatre.

Second production of *The Old Lady Says "No!"* by Dublin Gate Theatre in new home at the Rotunda Building, Dublin.

Appointed director of the Dublin Gate Theatre, position held until 1936.

1932   New York premiere of *The Moon in the Yellow River.*

1933   Premiere of *A Bride for the Unicorn,* Dublin Gate Theatre.

Writes screenplay for first Irish film, *Guests of the Nation.*

1934   Premiere of *Storm Song* at Dublin Gate Theatre.

American premiere of *A Bride for the Unicorn,* Harvard Dramatic Club, Cambridge.

Third Irish (Gate) production of *The Old Lady Says "No!"*

1935   Fourth Irish (Gate) production of *The Old Lady Says "No!"*

American premiere of *The Old Lady Says "No!"* Amherst College, Massachusetts.

English premiere of *The Old Lady Says "No!"* Westminster Theatre, London.

1936   At author's request, Johnston rewrites Ernst Toller's *Die Blinde Göttin,* produced as *Blind Man's Buff,* Abbey Theatre.

1936   Moves to Belfast to become Features Programme Writer and Director for the BBC, position held until 1938.

1937   Writes screenplays for Irish films: *River of Unrest* and *Ourselves Alone.*

1938   Television producer for BBC London until 1940.
        Fifth Irish (Gate) production of *The Old Lady Says "No!"* Cork Opera House.

1939   Premiere of *The Golden Cuckoo,* Longford Productions of the Dublin Gate Theatre.

1940   Premiere of *The Dreaming Dust* in the Gaiety Theatre (Gate Theatre production).

1940   Appointed to Irish Academy of Letters.
        Writer, broadcaster, and director until 1942 for BBC, London and Manchester.

1941   Theatre critic for Belfast periodical, *The Bell.*
        Sixth Irish (Gate) production of *The Old Lady Says "No!"* Gaiety Theatre, Dublin.

1942   BBC war correspondent until 1945 in Middle East, Italy, France, and Germany.

1945   Divorces Shelagh Richards and marries Betty Chancellor at Dungannon; two sons by second marriage, Jeremy and Rory.
        Awarded the Order of the British Empire.
        Appointed Programme Director of BBC television service, position held until 1947.

1947   Moves to New York to become scriptwriter for Theatre Guild of the Air, position held until 1949.

1948   Writes *A Fourth for Bridge.*
        North American tour of Dublin Gate Theatre, including United States and Canada; eighth production of *The Old Lady Says "No!"*

1950   Teaches at Amherst College.
        American premiere of *The Golden Cuckoo*, Provincetown, Massachusetts.

1950   Teaches English at Mount Holyoke College, Massachusetts, position held until 1960.

1953   Publishes *Nine Rivers from Jordan*, English edition; revised American edition published 1955.

1954   American premiere of *The Dreaming Dust*, Provincetown.

1955   Guggenheim Fellowship.
        Radio adaptation of *The Old Lady Says "No!"* for Radio Eireann.

1956   Writes and directs for Dublin Festival *Táin Bo Cuailgne: A Pageant of the Great Cattle Raid of Cooley and of the High Deeds of Cuchulainn, Champion of Ulster*.
        First production of *Strange Occurrence on Ireland's Eye*, Abbey Theatre.

1957   Production of *The Old Lady Says "No!"* Wesleyan University, Connecticut.
        Ninth Irish (Gate) production of *The Old Lady Says "No!"* Dublin Festival.

1958   First productions of *The Scythe and the Sunset*, Cambridge, Massachusetts, and Abbey Theatre, Dublin.

1959   Libretto for Hugo Weisgall's opera *Six Characters in Search of an Author;* New York City Opera, Lincoln Center premiere.
        Publication of *In Search of Swift*, controversial biography of Jonathan Swift.

1960   Publication of complete plays; American edition (Little, Brown), *The Old Lady Says "No!"* and *Other Plays* (1 vol.); British edition (Jonathan Cape), *Collected Plays* (2 vols.).

1960   Appointed head of Theatre and Speech Department, Smith College, Massachusetts; position held until 1966.

	Production of *The Old Lady Says "No!"* Melbourne, Australia (Marlowe Society).
1964	BBC television production (adapted without author's supervision) of *The Old Lady Says "No!"*
1966–67	Visiting Professor (Theatre), Amherst College.
1967–68	Visiting Theatre Director, University of Iowa.
1970–71	Visiting Professor (English), University of California, Davis.
1971–72	Berg Professor, New York University.
1972–73	Arnold Professor, Whitman College, Walla Walla, Washington.
1976	Visiting Director, Graduate Drama Centre, University of Toronto.
1977	Publication of *The Dramatic Works* (Vol. 1), Colin Smythe, Ltd., England. Tenth Irish production of *The Old Lady Says "No!"* Abbey Theatre.
1978	Publication of *The Brazen Horn: A Non-Book for Those Who, In Revolt Today, Could Be In Command To-Morrow;* published privately 1968. Litt. D. (*Honoris Causa*), University of Ulster.
1979	Publication of *The Dramatic Works* (Vol. 2), Colin Smythe, Ltd.
1984	Dies in Dublin, 8 August.

Note: Omitted from this chronology are Johnston's dozens of radio and television plays as well as most of his nondramatic writings. For the best bibliography of his work, see "Check List: Denis Johnston's Writings," *Denis Johnston: A Retrospective,* ed., Joseph Ronsley (Gerrards Cross: Colin Smythe, 1981), pp. 245–62.

INTRODUCTION

I. HISTORICAL AND POLITICAL CONTEXTS

In 1803 young Robert Emmet, Ireland's most romantic revolutionary hero, flung a challenge to his compatriots. In 1926 another young Dubliner, Denis Johnston, took up Emmet's gage. Before his execution Emmet had proclaimed:

> Let no man write my epitaph until other times and other men can do justice to my character. . . . When my country takes her place among the nations of the earth, then, and not till then, let my epitaph be written.

Inspired by Emmet's eloquent speech from the dock, revolutionary politics, and blighted love, many Irish writers have attempted, in their various ways, to "do justice" to his character. With the establishment of the Irish Free State in 1921, it seemed, at last, time to write the long-awaited epitaph. But Johnston thought differently. Deciding that his country had not yet achieved nationhood, he set about writing a play that would show his audience the way. Then, nothing daunted, he rewrote the sacred dock speech itself. This he presented at the end of his first play, *The Old Lady Says "No!"* produced at the Dublin Gate Theatre in 1929.

The title of the play sounded an alarming note, given how reverently Mother Ireland was usually treated in patriotic speeches, Emmet's included. Yet the historical Emmet might have been pleased with Johnston's dock speech, although the play's vision of the newborn nation could not have been reassuring. Johnston gave his Emmet a chance to unburden himself on the subject of the modern Irish: "Race of men with dogs' heads. Panniers filled with tripes and guts. . . . I have done with you."

Notwithstanding this vituperation, the play has always been highly regarded in Ireland. If the play has bewildered or

1

angered some of its audiences, others have honored it as one of the great Irish plays of the century.[1] From the time of its first production the play has been considered "extraordinary":[2] "No Irishman has ever written a play remotely resembling this," said one viewer, adding ambiguously, "and it is certainly an act of courage on the part of the directors of the Gate to present it on an Irish stage."[3] One man condemned the play as blasphemous, insisting that it put itself "outside the law of God and the law of the land";[4] another hated its "language of the gutter";[5] one critic simply confessed bafflement—not surprising, given the play's avant-garde dramatic form and host of learned allusions: "If 'E. W. Tocher'[6] intended merely to mystify his audience with his first play . . . he certainly went a long way towards success."[7] But not all viewers felt bewilderment or spleen. One of the critics declared "E. W. Tocher" the equal of John Millington Synge, and possessor of the "most richly equipped and modern a mind" in Irish drama.[8]

Even this brief sample of reaction reveals the background to a much more recent assessment: "Today *The Old Lady Says "No!"* still stands unchallenged as the most exciting play ever staged in Ireland; in 1929 its impact was enormous, and the [newly formed] Gate Theatre was mapped on the consciousness of the general public from then on."[9] The excitement was due in part to the audience's realization that they were present at an historic moment in Irish theatre history. In *The Old Lady,*

1. Harold Ferrar, *Denis Johnston's Irish Theatre* (Dublin: Dolmen, 1973), 15. Micheál ÓhAodha, *Theatre in Ireland* (Oxford: Basil Blackwell, 1974), 122. Vivian Mercier, "Perfection of the Life or of the Work?," *Denis Johnston, A Retrospective*, ed. Joseph Ronsley (Gerrards Cross: Colin Smythe, 1981), 243.

2. D. S. [David Sears] of the *Irish Independent*, 6 July 1929. Reviews of all Johnston's plays in their several productions are among the Johnston papers in the library of the University of Ulster at Coleraine, Northern Ireland.

3. *Daily Express*, 3 July 1929.

4. James O'Reilly, *Irish Statesman*. O'Reilly, a Dublin barrister, threatened to bring legal action for blasphemy against Johnston.

5. Unsigned, unpublished letter submitted to the *Irish Independent*, 5 February 1931, now among Johnston's papers at Trinity College Dublin Library.

6. Johnston's pen name until 1936 when he gave up practicing law. His real identity, however, seems to have been commonly known to Dublin theatre-goers, judging from the newspaper references. Johnston's diary explains the genesis of this name; in a humorous mood, he borrowed it off a Dublin marquée advertising an evangelical preacher of this name (3rd Omnibus: 1924–1934, p. 94).

7. *Evening Mail*, 4 July 1929.

8. C. P. Curran, *Irish Statesman*, 13 July 1929.

9. "Portrait Gallery," *Irish Times*, 17 October 1953.

they were seeing for the first time a play that transmuted the great contemporary experiments of international theatre into an Irish form and idiom. This transmutation remains the play's hallmark.

But there was another reason for the excitement caused by the play. Johnston gave a clue to this reaction when he responded publicly to the charge that it inflicted on the audience the playwright's private and rather vulgar nightmares:[10] "This play, if plays must be about something, is about what Dublin has made a good many of us feel. And if it is a very wrong and vulgar feeling that could only have been experienced by people with nasty minds, we aren't worth bothering about anyway. But it is no good saying that it isn't true, because we happen to know that it is."[11] Years later he put this more succinctly: "*The Old Lady* gave public expression to all I had to say about Dublin and her damned politics."[12]

Johnston was not the only writer raising a voice of protest against what Dublin was making them feel, nor was he the only Dubliner who did not scruple to equate Dublin with the rest of the country. In his disappointment, Johnston belonged to the generation that had come to maturity in the 1920s, just after Ireland had achieved its Free State status after centuries of English rule. The reality of that political emancipation revealed what a friend of Johnston called "the apathy, the futility, and the opportunism which had followed the achievement of a purpose too long cherished to the exclusion of nearer duties."[13]

These young people were electrified by the production in 1923 of Sean O'Casey's first play, *The Shadow of a Gunman*. This play exhibited a state of mind conditioned by the Anglo-Irish War of 1919–21 and the Civil War that followed in 1922–23. As Denis Johnston commented years later, it was

10. In his diary, *Record: 1924–1932* 8, p. 230, Johnston reports that these sentiments were expressed by Sir Philip and Lady [Deena Tyrell] Hanson, the latter of whom is pilloried in the play in the character of Lady Trimmer.

11. "A Note on What Happened." This essay, in slightly longer form, was written as Program notes for the first American presentation of the play, produced by Curtis Canfield at Amherst College, Massachusetts, 16 May 1935. The note is included in this edition, pp. 125–31.

12. "An Interview with Denis Johnston," conducted by Gordon Henderson, *Journal of Irish Literature* 2, nos. 2, 3 (May–September 1973), 33.

13. W. P. MacDonagh, "Trial by Drama," an unpublished short story dramatizing the author's reaction to the first production of *The Old Lady*, now among Johnston's papers at Trinity College Library.

"the first time we had heard expressed on the stage emotions that we were as yet hardly conscious of feeling ourselves."[14]

The Civil War was one of Ireland's most bitter periods, with former comrades-in-arms during the Anglo-Irish War now deadly enemies. The majority, who had accepted the 1921 Treaty granting British Dominion status to a partitioned Ireland, were condemned by the Irish Republican Army "Diehards," who were willing to accept nothing less than a Republic of the whole island. But the seeds of this Civil War had been germinating since before 1803. And they had been carefully nourished by a sentimentalized legend of Robert Emmet, who had come to represent in ballads, stories, and plays[15] an ideal of the doomed revolutionary hero in the service of the "Poor Old Woman" or Shan Van Vocht, symbol of subject Ireland. Emmet's abortive Dublin insurrection of 1803 was the final flicker of the great United Irishman Rising of 1798. With two of its leaders, Sir Edward FitzGerald and Wolfe Tone, just to name those conjured up in *The Old Lady Says "No!"*, Robert Emmet became an early and beloved exemplar in a long catalogue of violent Irish heroes.

So powerful was this ideal that Patrick Pearse (1879–1916), leader of the 1916 Easter Rising, would use it to mobilize the Irish with an apotheosis of Emmet's action: "No failure . . . was ever more complete, more pathetic than Emmet's. And yet he has left us a . . . memory of a sacrifice Christ-like in its perfection. . . . This man was faithful even unto the ignominy of the gallows, dying that his people might live, even as Christ died. . . . Be assured that such a death always means a redemption."[16]

This symbol of patriotic self-sacrifice had been put into an influential literary form in W. B. Yeats's 1902 play *Cathleen ni Houlihan*. Here the Poor Old Woman is transformed into a young woman with the "walk of a queen" when young men are willing to die for her cause. The cause was—and at the end of the twentieth century still is—the recovery of her "four beautiful green fields," the provinces of ancient Ireland: Leinster, Munster, Connacht, and Ulster. This dramatic image of political martyrdom, sweetened with sublimated eroticism, helped

14. "Plays of the Quarter," *Bell* 2:1 (April 1941), 90.
15. For a study of plays based on the Emmet story, see Harold Ferrar, "Robert Emmet in Irish Drama," *Eire-Ireland* 1:2 (1966), 19–28.
16. *How Does She Stand?* (Dublin: The Bodenstown Series, 1915), 9–10.

fuel a heedless patriotism available to Patrick Pearse in his call to arms: ". . . bloodshed is a cleansing and a sanctifying thing. . . . I would see any and every body of Irish citizens armed . . . [even though] we may make mistakes at first and shoot the wrong people."[17]

The results of such mythologizing were graphically displayed in O'Casey's *The Shadow of a Gunman*, where the sacred figure of Kathleen is redefined in the light of the Troubles "she" had caused:

> DAVOREN I remember the time when you yourself believed in nothing but the gun.
>
> SHEAMAS Ay, when there wasn't a gun in the country; I've a different opinion now when there's nothin' but guns in the country. . . . An' you daren't open your mouth, for Kathleen ni Houlihan is very different now to the woman who used to play the harp an' sing "Weep on, weep on, your hour is past," for she's a raging devil now, an' if you only look crooked at her you're sure of a punch in th' eye. . . .[18]

O'Casey's vision of Kathleen as devil was not original to him; Lady Augusta Gregory's journal reports two other Irish writers, George Russell [AE] and Lennox Robinson expressing the same heresy by 1922.[19] But Johnston found O'Casey's play useful in the way it located the source of betrayal in the love of violence promulgated in Irish drama and poetry, as well as in the stirring political oratory of the previous century.

Johnston's sense of outrage against Kathleen took a form very different from O'Casey's tragic realism. Humorously playing with the idea that the Irish have a special "affinity to drama" because they "like to talk,"[20] Johnston offered his audience a homeopathic cure. *The Old Lady Says "No!"* is a jumble of Dublin talk—the literary, political, religious, journalistic, and demotic speech of a city with a corporate personality and a long memory. Its dream play structure ruptures the conventions of predictable social discourse and, by this method, reveals how irrational and hollow that discourse could be in

17. *Collected Works: Political Writings and Speeches* (Dublin: Phoenix, 1917), 98–99.
18. *Collected Plays*, 4 vols. (London: Macmillan, 1949), 1:131–32.
19. *Lady Gregory's Journals 1916–1930*, ed. Lennox Robinson (London: Putnam and Co., 1946), 173–74.
20. "Interview with Denis Johnston," p. 43.

modern Dublin. Johnston organized a good deal of the dialogue into surrealistic pastiches of favorite Irish quotations —which by the 1920s were merely self-dramatizing imitations of lubricious language. The characters of *The Old Lady* play actors donning familiar roles and mouthing familiar language gone amuck. As Johnston wryly explained: "When asked by an English journalist 'just who is this Kathleen-ni-Houlihan' . . . I can only stammer confusedly that Miss Houlihan is a well-known Abbey Theatre actress. . . ."[21]

The play is not just satiric, however. In all his writings Johnston usually had more than one thing on his mind and did not seem to mind self-contradiction, a habit that causes confusion even in the most alert audience. He hoped to create an audience "that does not object to being left in some doubt as to what side it is on."[22] In this play, for example, he satirized the glamor of revolutionary politics with its disastrous effects on the modern spirit, even as he admitted the potency of revolutionary ideals. Johnston always maintained that "life itself is violent" and so he had to devise a religious creed and an art that could combine the "exhilarating fact of conflict with the god-like grace of Pity."[23] More specifically, in this play he was attempting to express "on the stage the idea of the triumph of the Word over environment," which he equated with the "dogma of the Resurrection."[24] So while puncturing the posture of romantic patriotism, he celebrated in the final scene a purified version of the Emmet story, one that verged on the Patrick Pearse model. Johnston somewhat ambiguously elevated Emmet into a figure of divine madness who believes in "the might of Creation, the majesty of the Will, the resurrection of the Word, and Birth Everlasting." In the smithy of his dream, Dublin, the "Strumpet City," "will walk the streets of Paradise."

Johnston's private diaries of the 1920s reveal how well he understood the suffering of the visionary who must struggle with warring sentiments in his own mind. As a playwright he

21. This quotation comes from the original version of "A Note on What Happened," now in Trinity College Manuscript Collection (see n. 11). He excised this quotation in the 1977 Colin Smythe, Ltd. edition of *Dramatic Works* 1.

22. "Introduction," *The Golden Cuckoo and Other Plays* (London: Jonathan Cape, 1954), 7.

23. "A Decade in Retrospect: 1939–49," *Month*, 3:2 (1950), 91–94.

24. "A Note on What Happened."

also knew how difficult it is to express this internal phenomenon on the stage. He solved this technical problem by peopling *The Old Lady* with the many shades of thought quarrelling in the mind of his dreaming central character whom he called the "Speaker." Most prominent among these is the talking statue of Henry Grattan, the great Irish parliamentarian (1746–1820) whose career-long struggle for the legislative independence of the Irish Parliament was destroyed by the Rebellion of 1798 led, as the statue puts it, by "omniscient young Messiahs with neither the ability to work nor the courage to wait." In *The Old Lady Says "No!"* Grattan confronts Emmet. But this struggle is primarily between Denis Johnston, the rational young barrister, and the fiery young playwright, "E. W. Tocher."

II. BIOGRAPHICAL AND THEATRICAL CONTEXTS

By background and training Denis Johnston found congenial Henry Grattan's rational use of parliamentary process based on English common law. Johnston's Scots-Irish Presbyterian parents were born in the north of Ireland; his father eventually became a Supreme Court justice of the Irish Free State. A Dubliner by birth, Johnston was a somewhat alien although prominent citizen of the south. Born on 18 June 1901[25] he was educated at elite private schools in Dublin and Edinburgh, then attended Christ's College, Cambridge. While at Cambridge, he was swept into office as president of the Cambridge Union after a single speech in which he excoriated the British deployment in Ireland, during the Anglo-Irish War of 1919–21, of auxiliary terrorist troops called the Black and Tans. With these activities he was preparing for what he thought would be a life in British politics.

Further law studies resulted in his being called to the Bars of England, Ireland, and Northern Ireland, and he continued to practice law, first in England, then Dublin, until 1936. But as early as 1924 his political and legal activities were second to his great interest—the theatre. And by the early 1930s, his impressively large and dazzling body of dramatic writing made him appear to many as the contemporary bright light of the Irish stage.

25. Most of the following biographical information was found in Johnston's diaries; some was supplied by Denis Johnston in interview or by letter; the rest is from Joseph Ronsley of McGill University.

After this decade of combining two successful careers, Johnston left Dublin to try the new medium of television (and to escape a damaging marriage breakup). In 1936 he started work with the BBC in Belfast. Shortly thereafter, he went to London where he became the first to write original scripts for British television

When World War II put an end to developmental work at the BBC he spent three years (1942–45) as a war correspondent for the BBC, first in the Middle East, then, moving with the Allied armies, in Italy, France, and Germany. The rich harvest of his wartime experiences appeared in the play *A Fourth for Bridge* and in his superb war memoir, *Nine Rivers from Jordan: The Chronicle of a Journey and a Search*. The theological and philosophical concerns of *Nine Rivers* were eventually expanded in his last book, *The Brazen Horn*.

After the war Johnston returned to London and the BBC, where he was appointed head of programmes. Despite the substantial amount of dramatic writing he was doing for the BBC and his influential position in its hierarchy, he left for New York in 1947 to become play adaptor for the New York Theatre Guild of the Air and director of its first television play broadcast.

From 1950 till retirement age in 1966 he undertook yet another career: university teaching. Throughout his long life he continued writing, although he wrote no plays after 1960.[26]

Even this brief summary of Johnston's personal history, intersecting in such significant ways with major events and developments of the twentieth century, supports Vivian Mercier's assertion that "we cannot deny Denis Johnston 'perfection of the life.'" But Mercier claims that we must acknowledge also "perfection of the work" in *The Old Lady Says "No!"*, *The Moon in the Yellow River*, and *Nine Rivers from Jordan*.[27] That Denis Johnston's first dramatic work might qualify as a "perfect work" is a remarkable claim, but Johnston had schooled himself very carefully for its composition.

With characteristic self-irony he explained that he decided to write plays because the writing of dialogue required neither

---

26. For a list of Johnston's writings see the "Checklist" in *Denis Johnston: A Retrospective*, compiled by Joseph Ronsley (Gerrards Cross: Colin Smythe, 1981), 245–62.

27. *Denis Johnston, A Retrospective*, p. 243.

research nor grammar and because "I like the company and conversation of actors and actresses—particularly the latter, two of whom I married, although not at the same time." He also suggested, more helpfully, that he wrote his own plays because he found it more and more difficult as a director of plays to find the kind he enjoyed handling.[28]

He had seen a great many plays in his life, since Dublin was the home of the Abbey Theatre and, by Johnston's time, internationally famous for its presentation of Irish drama. Beyond his regular attendance there, however, he had travelled extensively in Europe, particularly in Germany, where he had had the opportunity of witnessing great expressionist dramas with their innovative production methods. His lifelong interest in the theatre became a passion in 1923–24, the year he attended Harvard and frequented whenever possible the little theatres of Boston as well as the productions of the New York stage. In 1926, while maintaining residence in England in order to qualify for the English Bar,[29] he continued his education in theatre. London's fare at that time included the experimental London Gate Theatre, whose founder, Peter Godfrey, was able to circumvent the state censorship by maintaining his theatre as a private club and thus presenting plays considered too dangerous for the commercial theatre.[30] Johnston attended the Gate at least once with Sean O'Casey. Their education at the Gate in expressionist methods would flower within the year in Johnston's *Shadowdance* and by 1928 in O'Casey's *The Silver Tassie*.

These years were, as Johnston put it in a retrospective radio broadcast,

> . . . a time of very exciting developments in theatre, when many new types of writing were being attempted, and the world seemed to be full of plays that one wanted to see. Apart from the Tchekovs, Strindbergs, and Ibsens, there was a whole new crop of dramatists who had swum up

28. "Opus One," *The Old Lady Says "No!"*, p. 00.
29. He lived at the Bloomsbury Club, "a social and residential club for young men," hence this name as first place of composition listed at the end of the play. He made his last revisions to the play in 1977 while living at Dalkey, Ireland.
30. When *The Old Lady* was produced at the Westminster Theatre in London by the Dublin Gate in June 1935, the Lord Chamberlain's office had to review the play before granting it a license. The censor's letter, now among Johnston's papers at Trinity College, permitted production only after he deleted such words as "Jesus," "Christ," "God blast," "bastard" and, curiously, "half" the occurrences of "bloody."

into view since the First War. There were Benevente and the Sierras in Spain, the Capeks in Prague, Kaiser and Toller in Germany, Eugene O'Neill in the United States.[31] This list is helpful in two ways. It points to some of the places where Johnston found useful devices for his own first play: the structure of August Strindberg's *Dream Play*; expressionistic techniques from Ernst Toller and Georg Kaiser; the ironic treatment of the search for a Land of Heart's Desire in Josef Capek's *The Land of Many Names*; and a central dreamer in Eugene O'Neill's *The Fountain*, a play that creates a vision of a promised land in the final scene. But the list is important in another way, as it suggests the activity of the Dublin Drama League. Johnston joined this group after his return from the United States in 1924. It provided him with an apprentice's workshop in which to practice acting and directing.

The Drama League was a partly amateur, partly professional group founded in 1918 by Lennox Robinson and W. B. Yeats expressly to educate Dubliners in contemporary non-Irish plays. The League was given the Abbey stage on Sunday and Monday nights when the regular theatre was dark. The group put on a play a month for the six months of the regular season, each new play running for two nights.[32]

In his radio talk, Johnston described the eager participation of Dubliners in theatre of any sort, an enthusiasm he both shared and parodied in act 2 of *The Old Lady Says "No!"*, where he catalogued some of Dublin's groups:

MINISTER [OF ARTS AND CRAFTS] Are you interested in Art, Mr. Emmet?

LADY TRIMMER I suppose you're a member of the Nine Arts Club?

WIFE And the Royal Automobile Academy?

CHORUS Celebrity Concerts, The Literary Literaries.

WIFE Perhaps he acts for the Civil Service Dramatics.

MINISTER (*confidentially*) Say the word and I'll get you into the Rathmines and Rathmines. I know the man below.

31. "The Dublin Drama League," 6–7, an unpublished typescript of a radio talk now among Johnston's papers at The University of Ulster at Coleraine, Northern Ireland. Although undated, the internal and external evidence suggests that it dates from 1947 when Johnston was Radio Eireann's drama critic.

32. Denis Johnston, "The Making of the Theatre," in *The Gate Theatre: Dublin*, p. 12. See also Brenna Katz Clarke and Harold Ferrar, *Dublin Drama League 1918–1941* (Dublin: Dolmen, 1979).

If Johnston mocked the dilettantism of these antics, he was also well aware of the necessity for such ferment as the cultural milieu in which some great work might grow.[33] The amateurishness allowed the neophytes to take what he called in his radio broadcast the "easy-going initial steps."

Even the frequent activities of the Drama League were too few to please Johnston and his future wife Shelagh Richards, so in 1927 they formed the "Dramick," later called the New Players. It was this group that "actually staged Ireland's first expressionist productions in the drawing rooms of private houses with the aid of a set of curtains, wires, cardboard boxes, and sheets of beaver board worthy of Heath Robinson."[34]

In November 1927 he gave the city its first professional view of expressionist theatre in a New Players production of Georg Kaiser's *From Morn Till Midnight*.[35] This was also the first production to be staged in the Peacock Theatre, a 102-seat theatre built in the Abbey to accommodate this kind of experimental work. In April 1928 he directed a Drama League production of Eugene O'Neill's *The Fountain*. In November of 1928 he directed *King Lear*, the Abbey's first Shakespeare production.[36] Then in March 1929 he directed Ernst Toller's *Hopplà, Wir Leben!*, again for the Drama League.

By the time of the Toller production Johnston showed the confidence of a person determined to create a new epoch in the Irish theatre. Among the Johnston papers at Trinity College are letters from some of his *Hopplà* actors withdrawing from the production, afraid of the play's sexual and political boldness. One of those who remained was A. J. Leventhal, a Trinity College lecturer and one of the first Irish reviewers of Joyce's *Ulysses*.[37] This is how he remembered those events:

33. In a 1959 article Johnston explained that playwrighting is "essentially an art that flourishes only in some common ground or orchard, where one tree can cross-fertilize another. That is why in all countries, productive periods in the theatre are brought about by groups and cliques, with some form of common understanding as to who they are, and what they are after." "What Has Happened to the Irish," *Theatre Arts* 43 (July 1959), 11–12.

34. "The Making of the Theatre," pp. 13–14.

35. A list of the seventeen plays Johnston directed in Dublin between 1924–36 appears in *3rd Omnibus*, 219. At that time in Ireland the term for "director" was "producer," with the former title reserved for the directors of the theatre board.

36. For a discussion of this production, see Christopher Murray, "Early Shakespearean Productions by the Abbey Theatre," *Theatre Notebook* 33:2 (1979), 66–80.

37. Cited in Richard Ellmann, *James Joyce* (London: Oxford, 1965), 527.

Denis Johnston is right in recalling that various people withdrew their patronage and several actors refused parts. Partly I think because Toller was communist and partly because the central character is, according to the text, in bed with Eva Berg during their dialogue. Those were puritanical days in Dublin. . . . In a letter of thanks J. refers "to all the threats and mutterings and gloomy portendings that you were subjected to (for reasons still undiscovered)."[38]

Johnston's refusal to bow to the respectable was not just the young man's desire to *épater la bourgeoisie*; he was determined to make Dublin a place receptive to international currents. This project required determined knocking on some hallowed doors, particularly that of the Abbey.

During these years of amateur acting and directing, while he was also beginning to practice law, Johnston was already writing a play that he hoped would be produced at the Abbey Theatre. An October 1926 diary entry recorded his hopes and anxieties:

If I really knew that I was any good it would complete the metamorphosis [from lawyer to playwright]. . . . But if my play turns out in time to be worth the acting I will swing myself out of the last strands of childish diffidence. If not I will grin and write another and then another until—well until the world (very foolishly and with manifold short-sightedness) breaks me.[39]

The uncertain tone of these private musings did not sound in his combative public voice, however. Two years before the Toller production he had published in a Dublin newspaper a challenge to the Abbey directors—W. B. Yeats, Lady Gregory, Lennox Robinson, and Walter Starkie:

The Directors of the Abbey are undoubtedly in competition with the younger and less-established playwrights of the city, and however honest their motives, there will always be the tendency so long as the present system continues to put on such plays as "The Big House" [by Lennox Robinson] or "Oedipus Rex" [by W. B. Yeats] in preference to

---

38. Letter to Christine St. Peter, 26 April 1979, Paris, France.
39. *Record* 8, p. 146. This and Johnston's other diaries are among Johnston's papers at Trinity College.

the work of Mr. [F. J.] O'Hare and his friends. It is not, I repeat, conscious unfairness. It is merely Human Nature.[40]

This is a bold letter for an *ingénu* playwright to address to those holding his fate in the balance—especially as his diary contains an official acknowledgment of the Abbey's receipt of his first play, dated 3 March 1927, less than a month after this newspaper challenge.[41]

Johnston's self-assurance left the editor of the newspaper spluttering. In the same day's issue, under Johnston's letter, he responded:

> We think it preposterous to substitute for such famous and experienced dramatists as Lady Gregory, W. B. Yeats and Lennox Robinson, people who are not writers at all, who have no experience of stagecraft. . . . [S]omebody ought to tie these people's heads in a bag where their folly may affect only themselves.

This exchange is the opening salvo in the very public controversy that eventually surrounded Johnston's play and created an audience eager for its arrival. But in the spring of 1927 his relations with the Abbey directors continued peaceably despite his brash letter.

In April he returned temporarily from England, where he was still practicing law, to act in *The Constant Nymph*. On 23 April Lennox Robinson returned his script, at that time entitled *Shadowdance*, with the instructions to cut the two-act play to one act, since "the Abbey Directors say that the audience cannot be expected to stand more than seventy minutes of this sort of thing."[42] Johnston's diary records that he immediately set about revising the play according to Robinson's directions and resubmitted it in one-act form within two months. On 30 June Robinson wrote to Johnston: "WBY has been up for a day and very busy over 'Shadowdance'—cutting here and cutting there—God help you. But he wants to see the original version —thinks I was wrong to make you cut all the Dáil [scene in act 1]—so can you send it to him?"[43]

40. *Irish Statesman*, 5 February 1928.

41. *3rd Omnibus*, p. 85

42. *Record 8*, p. 171. Johnston also discusses this rejection on p. 183 of the diary. In the first reference, he crossed out the name "Lennox" and wrote "Yeats" above it; in the second entry he did not substitute Yeats's name.

43. Unpublished letter from Lennox Robinson to Denis Johnston in Trinity College Manuscripts Collection.

Johnston's diary remains silent for a year on the subject of the play's reception. Then in October 1928 he angrily noted the Abbey's definitive rejection of his play:

I saw red and started to put it back into two parts—worse and more unbearable parts than ever before. All I knew or ever felt or heard or experienced about Ireland I put into that play until, when I had finished it again, I felt that never again would I be able to write another play. . . . I retitled it "Rhapsody in Green" and there it is.[44]

But the story had other complications Johnston was unaware of, recorded in letters exchanged among the directors. Both Yeats and Robinson had obviously led Johnston to believe that they were seriously interested in producing his play, so after their rejection, they tried to soften the blow by promising Johnston a fifty-pound subsidy if he would produce the play at another theatre. They also offered Johnston the opportunity to direct *King Lear* in November 1928. But they made these decisions without consulting their fellow directors, and Lady Gregory objected to having theatre business conducted in this way.[45] After a small flurry of letters (17, 26 November; 27 December 1928) in which Yeats insisted that these decisions had been taken at a directors' meeting, he wrote an apologetic recantation on 21 January 1929 explaining his actions: "You must wonder why Lennox and I are pushing Dennys Johnson [*sic*]. My reason (and I think Lennox supports me in it) is that if we do not train our successors the theatre will fall into the hands of Con Curran or worse. I am thinking of Dennys Johnson as a possible director [administrator] of the theatre."[46]

Robinson unquestionably supported Yeats in this plan and was probably the instigator of it. In a letter to Yeats written on 3 January 1930 before Yeats had yet seen Johnston's *King Lear*, which was about to be revived, Robinson tried to reopen the discussion of Johnston's appointment: "When you were 44 and I was 22 you made me Manager and Producer. I am now 44 and I feel we should look for a young man of 22. . . . I can think of no one but Denis Johnston and I ask you to consider whether

44. *Record* 8, p. 201.

45. *Journals 1916–1930*, ed. Lennox Robinson (London: Putnam and Co., 1946), 112–13.

46. Unpublished letter from W. B. Yeats to Lady Augusta Gregory, National Library of Ireland, Ms. 18746.

he should not be made a Director."[47] But when Yeats saw Johnston's *Lear* with its expressionist staging and lighting, he hated it,[48] just as he had earlier balked at the expressionist devices of *Shadowdance*.

Rumor would have it—rumor often published as fact[49] —that Lady Gregory was responsible for the Abbey rejection of Johnston's play, and that the rejected *Shadowdance* typescript was returned to him with the words "the old lady says no" scrawled across the front of the title page. Since "the old lady" was the name some of the Abbey company irreverently used for Lady Gregory, she would, according to this rumor, be the villain of the plot. Again private letters and journals tell a different story.

Lennox Robinson had written to Johnston on 12 August 1928 telling him that the revised play "goes tomorrow to Lady Gregory for Yeats goes there tomorrow and she can read it to him. . . . I am for doing it—quite strongly for doing it—it is better now without the Dail scene and I hope we'll be able to let you know definitely in a few weeks time."[50]

Then on 14 August 1928 Lady Gregory copied into her journal a letter she had just written to Robinson telling him that after reading the revised play to Yeats she had come to agree with Yeats's negative assessment. It was the play's uncongenial (and misnamed) form that was, apparently, its important flaw:

> Yeats had said 'I told G.B.S. [George Bernard Shaw] the other day that perhaps I ought not to judge plays but give place to someone else as I don't know about impressionism' and he said 'There is nothing in it, in impressionism.'
>
> I asked Yeats then 'What is impresionism' and he said 'no law'—and I said 'all jaw' and he said 'Just so.' And that certainly describes this play.[51]

A 17 November 1928 letter from Yeats to Lady Gregory verifies her journal entry, as he reminded her that "You and Lennox,

---

47. *Letters to W. B. Yeats* 2, ed. Richard J. Finneran, George Mills Harper, and William M. Murphy (London: Macmillan, 1977), 501.

48. Murray, 72.

49. See, for example, the *Irish Literary Supplement* (Fall 1985), 6.

50. Unpublished letter from Robinson to Johnston, Trinity College Manuscripts Collection.

51. *Lady Gregory's Journals*, ed. Daniel J. Murphy (Gerrards Cross, Eng.: Colin Smythe, 1987), 2:307.

Lennox especially, had been anxious to be producing the play
—when you and I read it *the last time* however you agreed with
me about it."[52]

If Yeats was a primary force in the rejection, how did
Lady Gregory get the blame? Johnston himself was responsible
—at first in anger, then in a spirit of mischief that has provided
him with one of the most memorable titles in Irish drama. To
Johnston the final insult the Abbey dealt his play was their
refusal to honor the promised fifty-pound subsidy. In an October 1928 diary entry Johnston recorded Yeats's claim that he
had "liked the play" but that the Abbey had decided to reject it
because "if we put on this play, we would annoy our audiences
and lose fifty pounds. . . . So we are prepared to give you the
fifty pounds to put it on yourself."[53] When Lady Gregory apparently objected to Yeats's unilateral decision, he backed off,
writing her on 17 November 1928 that "details were not gone
into but it was a guarantee not a free gift." But since Yeats was
in Rapallo, Italy, at the time, it was left to Lady Gregory to
inform Johnston of the change. Her way of doing this angered
him, since she told him she liked the opening playlet, whose
parody she apparently missed, but found the rest of the play
"common." Johnston's fury at her judgment spilled out in a
diary entry that also revealed how condescending the Abbey
was toward the Gate Theatre in 1928:

> Then of course came the business of getting the fifty
> pounds out of the Abbey. Oh indeed no, said the Abbey.
> We[54] only of course meant it as a guarantee. . . . Then
> their auditor, George Hill Tulloch [insisted that] the Gate,
> to qualify for the fifty pounds cover, must not spend more
> on this show than on any other show. Otherwise they
> might be tempted to have higher expenses in view of the
> guarantee and be more likely to lose. And to protect
> themselves . . . the Abbey must have the audited accounts
> of the . . . expenses of every other show to compare with
> the audited accounts and expense of this show and would
> only pay the losses up to fifty pounds insofar as the show
> was no more expensive than any other show. So seeing

52. Unpublished letter from Yeats to Lady Gregory, National Library of Ireland, Ms. 18745.
53. *Record* 8, p. 202.
54. The "we" here, which I copied in 1976, had been struck out when I checked it
in 1986 and the name "Yeats" substituted.

that the poor old Gate was not going to get a mill of any fifty pounds from the dear old Abbey or anything like it, I said to Lennox, oh hell, give us fifteen pounds in cash and be done with it—at which he simply leapt. So the play went into rehearsal and I spitefully changed the name to *The Old Lady Says "No!"*[55]

The youthful Johnston in his anger did not stop at attacking Lady Gregory with his title. He also included in the reconstructed two-act play much more abusive allusions to Yeats's *Cathleen ni Houlihan*. Since Yeats attended the opening night of *The Old Lady* in July 1929[56] he could not have been unaware of Johnston's attack. But Johnston's spleen did not deter the Abbey directors from producing *The Moon in the Yellow River* in 1931, a decision that assumes a continuing regard for his talent, although Yeats resisted a campaign in the mid-1930s to make Johnston the manager of the Abbey, saying, "Johnston is a young man who would want his own way."[57]

The story does not, however, end there. After Johnston's death in 1984, his papers were donated to Trinity College Library. Amongst them is the title page of a third typescript version of *Shadowdance*; this title is crossed out with the words "Sorry" and "The Old Lady Says No" written over the other title. Nicholas Grene noted that the words "The Old Lady Says No" were not written by someone at the Abbey, but by the Gate Theatre manager, Art O'Murnaghan. This typescript was the one used as the Gate's prompt copy, as is clearly written on it. Then Grene correctly guessed that the "Sorry" was added by Johnston himself who in a "mischievous mood doctored one of his own manuscripts to authenticate the anecdote."[58] In 1976 Johnston allowed me to photocopy his typescripts. At that time "Sorry" did not exist on this title page (or any page among Johnston's papers). If it is a pity to ruin a good story, the real story reveals how acute was Johnston's sense of betrayal and how shabbily he had been treated in this instance by the Abbey directors.

---

55. *Record* 8, p. 224–25.

56. Joseph Holloway, *Impressions of a Dublin Playgoer* (July–September 1929), vol. 1, Ms. 1927, p. 15, National Library of Ireland.

57. "Quarrelling with Yeats," in *W. B. Yeats: Interviews and Recollections*, ed. E. H. Mikhail (London: Macmillan, 1977), 2:345.

58. "Modern Irish Literary Manuscripts," *Treasures of the Library*, ed. Peter Fox (Dublin: Royal Irish Academy, 1986), 237.

In 1950 Thomas Hogan assessed their decision very harshly: "The Abbey directors were quite right in their opinion that *The Old Lady* was not their kind of play and, indeed, it might be said that this was the point where the Abbey stopped being the Irish National Theatre."[59]

Armed with the meager fifteen-pound subsidy from the Abbey, in 1929 Johnston passed his play over to Hilton Edwards, an English director who, with the brilliant Irish actor Micheál MacLiammóir, had created the Dublin Gate Theatre the previous year. They were actively looking for avant-garde, Irish-written plays. In *The Old Lady Says "No!"* they found a play, as MacLiammóir later recalled, that was

altogether remarkable and precisely the sort of Irish play we had been hoping for. . . . It read, as Hilton remarked, like a railway guide and played like *Tristan and Isolde*. It gave at least two magnificent acting parts, and the chance of a lifetime to the sort of producer Hilton was rapidly becoming, a producer who can handle choral speaking, rhythmical movement, metrical climax, and a magnificence of massed effect with the precision of a ballet-master.[60]

They produced the play in the Peacock Theatre at the end of the Gate's second season. It received "thunders of applause, showers of praise and abuse and had a prolonged run" with the "theatre booked out every night." For Edwards and MacLiammóir, the night of *The Old Lady*'s premiere was the end of their "shop-window days and we knew it."[61] They subsequently revived the play in Ireland eight times between 1931 and 1957, taking it as well to England and North America where, admittedly, the Irish allusions tended to baffle audiences.[62]

Given that the play required experience in expressionist production methods, the rejection of the play by the Abbey, with no experience in this genre, turned out to be fortunate. The sensational Gate production was the beginning of Johnston's reputation, and the launching of a serious rival for the

59. "Denis Johnston: The Last of the Anglo-Irish," *Envoy* 3:9 (August 1950), 34.

60. Micheál MacLiammóir, *All for Hecuba* (London: Methuen, 1946); rpt. *Denis Johnston: A Retrospective*, p. 5.

61. MacLiammóir, 9

62. As Johnston explained in his program notes to the 1977 Abbey production, virtually the only other productions of the play were in small theatre groups or university drama departments.

Abbey. As Christopher Murray points out: "In the years after 1930 the fortunes of the Abbey declined, while those of the newly founded Gate Theatre, for whom Johnston's *The Old Lady Says "No!"* was a spectacular success, rose rapidly." This success reportedly infuriated Yeats[63] perhaps in part because, even as late as 1932, he might have hoped to have Johnston as an Abbey director.[64] If this was Yeats's hope, it was subverted by Johnston's appointment in 1931 as a Gate director. To Johnston's lifelong regret,[65] he never became an Abbey director.

III. CRITICAL AND LITERARY CONTEXTS

Yeats's negative judgment was not just a reaction against the "no law" and "all jaw" of the play's expressionist techniques. From the letters and journals quoted above, it seems clear that the Abbey directors had not seen the two-act version Johnston recreated after their final rejection, the version that stands with minor revisions in this edition.[66] A study of the first two versions of the play reveals why Yeats might have found these of questionable value. They were floridly overwritten and, where satire was intended, too ambiguous. In the opening playlet where Robert comes out of hiding to bid adieu to his love Sarah Curran, Johnston's supposed satire of the Abbey's patriotic romances sounds as though he is aspiring to an imitation, not a parody, of some of the more sentimental Abbey plays. Moreover, Sarah's opening speech echoes almost verbatim a poem that Johnston wrote in his 1924 diary, apparently with serious intent. Understandable, then, that Lady Gregory recorded in her diary affection for this part that "sent her mind wandering through romantic historical alleys."[67] Yeats too had trouble perceiving the intended tone: on the second typescript he noted that "when I first read this scene I thought

---

63. Murray, 74–75.
64. Ann Saddlemyer establishes this probability from letters exchanged between George and W. B. Yeats, as for example in this statement on 29 February 1932: "[I]ncidentally, the fact that Denis Johnston is now a director of the Gate marks him off the list as a possible director of the Abbey!" *Omnium Gatherum: Essays for Richard Ellmann*, ed. Susan Dick, Declan Kiberd, Dugald Macmillan, and Joseph Ronsley, (Gerrards Cross: Colin Smythe, Ltd., 1989), 300.
65. *3rd Omnibus 1924–1934*, p. 217.
66. This clarity is muddied by a mistaken identification in *Lady Gregory's Journals* (2:630, n. 3), where the editor, Daniel J. Murphy, substitutes Johnston's Emmet play for one by Heinrich Federer, *Patria*.
67. Gregory, 62.

the ornate writing was deliberate caracature [sic], a parody of popular romance he saw elsewhere and with serious intent."[68]

If Johnston's first satiric writing misfired, his attempts to achieve stirring poetical declamation were ridiculous. The original dock speech, the play's climactic moment, Yeats's marginal comment declares as "rubbish."[69] Here again Johnston's rhetoric is similar to ruminations in his diary, as when he paraphrased Edward Fitzgerald's *Rubaiyat of Omar Khayyam* to reveal his own literary aspirations.[70] This is not to suggest that Johnston was uncritical of his own poetic efforts; at one point in his diary he describes them as "sickly sentimentality and unmanly mouthings."[71] But to criticize one's own failed poetry is one thing; to have one of the great poets of the language pillory it, quite another. As Johnston was to remark ruefully two decades later: "Whatever O'Casey may have said to the contrary, to have had a script parsed and caustically annotated by Yeats was an experience that no aspiring writer can profitably forget."[72]

Johnston's future dramatic and prose writing would thereafter show self-conscious withdrawal into irony or some other form of self-protection whenever he touched such lyric moments.[73] But in revising this play, Johnston did not just change his rhetoric. After Yeats's rough handling, all subsequent versions of the play intensified the satiric aspects of the play at the expense of the visionary. By the time of the 1977 Abbey production, Johnston considered the most up-to-date and convincing parts the lines of Grattan's statue deriding romantic Irish nationalism and those of the Blind Man orating on the folly of dreams.[74] This increased emphasis on the satiric

---

68. *Beta*, Verso, Leaf 3.

69. *Beta*, Leaf 51.

70. [13 October 1926] "For all I know I may still be some good yet—I may still take up life in both my hands and mould it nearer to my heart's desire. I may still get out of the bar. I may still find out that I can create." *Record 1924–32* 8, p. 145. Compare to stanza 73 of the *Rubaiyat* (London: Ballantine Press, 1901): "Ah love! Could thou and I / With fate conspire / To grasp this sorry scheme Of things entire / Would not we shatter it to / Bits—and then / Re-mould it nearer to the Heart's desire."

71. *Record* 8, p. 27.

72. "What Happened to the Irish," p. 72.

73. Raymond Williams (*Drama from Ibsen to Eliot* [Harmondsworth, Eng.: Penguin, 1964], 29) uses the final moments of Johnston's *The Moon in the Yellow River* as a prime example of the "fatal self-consciousness" he thinks afflicts twentieth-century European drama.

74. Letter to Christine St. Peter, 3 June 1977, Dalkey, Ireland.

blurs the effect of the Speaker's dock speech in the final moments of the play by undercutting its promise of transformation. Yet, as we shall see, Johnston had unquestionably intended the visionary and the satiric emphases when he began writing the play.

In choosing to accentuate the satiric, Johnston was, to a degree, also choosing a literary tradition. He professed to have always been unwilling to sit respectfully at the feet of Yeats;[75] after the *Shadowdance* skirmish Johnston turned to his more congenial literary forebears, Jonathan Swift and G. B. Shaw. Johnston claimed that Shaw had formed his thought processes and taught him "a scepticism of greatness and a profound dislike of anything that savours of magic."[76] This heightening of satire in the finished play gives rise in turn to a dominant type of critical approach to the play.

Dorothy Macardle's *Irish Press* review of the 1932 Cape edition of the play offers a good example of this type of criticism in its most extreme form: "[W]ith the exploitation of Emmet, Denis Johnston has gone further than most Irish writers would care to, perhaps. Bitterness against all revolutionaries seems to be the inspiration of the fantasy of *The Old Lady Says "No!"*"[77]

A more dispassionate and historical view was offered in 1962 by Vivian Mercier, who argued that this play is the "only work by an Abbey [*sic*] Theatre dramatist . . . which is integrally conceived as a satire."[78] Mercier convincingly places this play in the Swiftian tradition of "Irish satire in the English language," although one might query Mercier's claim that the play juxtaposes old Ireland with new Ireland in a way that permits the new to be judged inferior to the old. Johnston, in revealing the tawdriness of the new Ireland, discovers weaknesses in the old that are responsible for the modern poisoning of sensibility.

Robert Hogan, writing in 1967 about the importance of Johnston's "adult theatre" in the period after the "Irish Renaissance," also emphasized *The Old Lady*'s satiric focus.

75. "What Has Happened to the Irish," 72.
76. "George Bernard Shaw," *Irish Literary Portraits,* ed. W. R. Rodgers (London: B.B.B. Corporation, 1972), 116.
77. 14 November 1932.
78. *Irish Comic Tradition* (Oxford: Oxford University Press, 1962), 203.

He argued that the play's satire is located in the incongruous juxtaposition between Emmet's ideals and the modern sentimentalizing of that ideal; this creates an "effect of sardonic negation: the ideal has been punctured, the sentimental has been made to appear spurious and the tawdry emptiness has triumphed."[79]

Other critics agree with Hogan. Harold Ferrar in 1973 and Gene A. Barnett in 1978 both find the "main theme" of the play in "the dismal reality of the Irish situation in the twenties—revolt, civil war, assassination, atrocities—against the rage for sentiment—religious, political, cultural, emotional —which is precisely the source of self-perpetuating violence."[80]

This emphasis on the play's satire leads logically to a rejection of any positive interpretation of the final scene of the play. As Barnett put it, the Speaker's litany of curses makes it clear that his "condemnation does not spring from any degree of enlightenment but is merely a reaffirmation of his own dream and a rejection of any possible challenge to the dead past."[81] One of the play's first critics, Curtis Canfield, saw Emmet's curses as "proof enough for me that he is a destructive agency" and that the "survival of a patriotic ideal which demands that life be sacrificed for a cause is not only retrogressive in effect but wasteful and ridiculous."[82]

In 1981 D. E. S. Maxwell offered a more complex reading of the satire: "This swirling collage does not represent Glorious Past versus squalid present, though there is perhaps a note of lament for squandered innocence, self-deception uncovered. The play dramatises an instance of history's trick of repeating itself in an unprecedented, unforeseen idiom."[83] In speaking of the play's method, Maxwell pointed out that the play ends as it begins with borrowed words, and if "Words have the last word," they "gesture towards positions rather than fix the play in a

79. *After the Irish Renaissance: A Critical History of the Irish Drama since "The Plough and the Stars"* (Minneapolis: University of Minnesota Press, 1967), 135–36.

80. Ferrar, 19; Barnett, 26.

81. Barnett, 39–40.

82. "A Note on the Nature of Expressionism and Denis Johnston's Plays," in *Plays of Changing Ireland* (New York: Macmillan, 1936); rpt., *Denis Johnston: A Retrospective*, 41, 45.

83. "The Mill of the Mind: Denis Johnston," in *Modern Irish Drama* (Cambridge: Cambridge University Press, 1981); rpt. as "Waiting for Emmet," in *Denis Johnston: A Retrospective*, 33.

stance."[84] This observation about "positions" allows for a mul-
tivalent interpretation of the play's ending. Were the thunderous ending merely satiric, the play should be a theatrical failure
—and this has not been the story of its stage history.

The quotation from Maxwell points to another useful
type of critical study of the play—the difficult task of locating
and interpreting the dozens of allusions. Hogan maintained that
the play's "strong theatrical merits can hardly be fully appreci-
ated unless one has studied the playscript closely, chased down
many unfamiliar allusions, and understood their historical context." In 1967 he felt that the play repaid the effort and that its
theatrical effect was not diminished by its "dazzling reliance
upon allusion."[85] More recently, he has had second thoughts. In
1981 he wrote that Johnston had never been properly credited
for his originality in adapting to the drama the allusive tech-
nique of T. S. Eliot and James Joyce; still, Hogan felt that in the
1977 production of the play, "even this strong point appeared
weakish."[86] Maxwell, however, found more durable value in the
play's "remarkably effective blending of invention which looks
to cosmopolitan sources and a content which is parochial. The
parochial, unlike the provincial, has an assured sense of its identity, and latent universal implications readier to be delivered."[87]

Since the meaning and method of *The Old Lady* reside in
the play of allusions, many critics find it necessary to spend the
bulk of their discussions unravelling its richly allusive texture.
Ferrar's and Barnett's full-length studies of Johnston's drama
usefully identify a number of the allusions, although both discussions are otherwise slightly flawed by their reliance on Ferrar's
misinformation about the play's textual history and Abbey
reception.[88]

One other very fruitful type of criticism has existed since
the first production: the comments offered by theatre people
on the play's technical method. Here one finds almost universal
admiration for Johnston's theatrical genius and general agree-

---

84. Maxwell, 35.
85. Hogan, 134–35.
86. "Denis Johnston's Horse Laugh," in *Denis Johnston: A Retrospective*, 60.
87. Maxwell, 29.
88. Harold Ferrar claimed that "Yeats and Robinson were sympathetic [to the play], but not stubbornly enough to counter Lady Gregory's swift refusal." He also stated that there are only three extant versions of the play, an error that led to others in his discussion of the play's history. *Denis Johnston's Irish Theatre*, 12, 22.

ment with his statement that *The Old Lady* is a "director's play written very much in the spirit of 'Let's see what would happen' if we did this or that."[89] Curtis Canfield analyzed the musical structure; Richard Allen Cave, the unique transformation of expressionist conventions; John Boyd, Johnston's virtuosity in orchestrating "a collage of colour and scene, choral speaking, argot, cliché, quotation; swift 'cutting' between scenes; timeshifts; the shattering of illusion; the unconventional use of the stage itself; the unexpected tempi of the action."[90]

These theatre critics have been concerned primarily with how the play works on the stage. Important among them, therefore, are its first producer and lead actor, Hilton Edwards and Micheál MacLiammóir, who virtually owned the play for nearly half a century. Johnston once called their brilliant staging as integral to the play as his text.[91] For MacLiammóir the role of the Speaker remained the "most musically exhilarating" of his long acting career: "It gives one a sense of being a soloist in some gigantic concerto, ping on the note, and away you go and keep going until the orchestra crashes about you and then is silent again for your next big attack, and all in a dazzle of green light and black, blinding shadow."[92] But Richard Allen Cave cautions against the danger of canonizing this successful production, since repetition could diminish the play to the status of interesting "museum piece." Each generation must find a "new visual language" to unsettle the audience, to make them realize that "the nightmare [Johnston] is analysing is a continuing condition. . . ."[93] Cave judged that Tomás Mac Anna, who in 1977 directed the Abbey's only production of *The Old Lady*, succeeded in doing this.

Cave, and most critics, read the play's ending very differently from MacLiammóir and Edwards. Cave found in the final apostrophe to Dublin an absurd piece of rhetoric about an Eden regained,[94] whereas MacLiammóir glimpsed "gleams of worship as passionate as Padraic Pearse or as Emmet him-

89. "Opus One," *The Old Lady Says "No!"*, p. 52.
90. Canfield, 39–40; Cave, "Johnston, Toller and Expressionism," pp. 79–83; Boyd, "The Endless Search," p. 161, all in *Denis Johnston: A Retrospective.*
91. "Opus One," *The Old Lady Says "No!"*, p. 53.
92. MacLiammóir, 5.
93. Cave, 81.
94. Cave, 82.

self."[95] To Hilton Edwards, the finale achieves "thunderous soul-searching heights" in Johnston's "massive orchestration of his credo. . . ."[96] Given the prominence of the "Credo of the Invincibles" near the end of the play, Edwards's remark demands scrutiny.

In the only study of Johnston's complete literary *oeuvre*, Veronica O'Reilly in 1980 found evidence of Johnston's later theological and philosophical concerns already present in his first work. Specifically, she suggested that Johnston shared with his Speaker a belief in the importance of his prophetic role:

> The prophetic role remains at the end of this play, triumphant in its essence, but brutally stripped of the deadly folly that often accrues. The garden image, so central in Johnston's later writings, here adumbrates that place where developing and developed heroes/realists taste of the tree of the Knowledge of Good and Evil, taste death in the apple of experience, and then spit it out to begin another innocence beyond maturity.[97]

In the litany of curses that some critics find merely destructive, Johnston was reviving his favorite religious liturgy, the Commination Service of the Anglican Church. He was also echoing one of his most important intellectual models, William Blake's "Proverbs of Hell": "Damn braces. Bless relaxes."

In this light, the play has to be seen as both satiric and visionary, its finale a paean to the creative force of the human spirit. While it belongs to the satiric tradition, *The Old Lady* fits as well into what Herbert Howarth described as the tradition of Irish literary messianism.[98] When asked, for example, why he had used the word "romantic" in his subtitle, Johnston explained:

> I called it romantic because it was a play about the search for the place where dreams come true, the land of Tir-na-n'Og. I was playing with the idea that if a person says the dream often enough, it comes true. . . . The Irishmen's dream did create the Republic. . . . Perhaps in spite of my-

95. "Problem Plays," in *The Irish Theatre*, ed. Lennox Robinson (London: Macmillan, 1939), 217.

96. "An Appreciation," in *Denis Johnston: A Retrospective*, 1–2.

97. "Vision and Form in the Works of Denis Johnston," unpublished Ph.D. dissertation for the University of Toronto, 1980, p. 99.

98. *The Irish Writers 1880–1940: Literature under Parnell's Star* (London: Rockcliff, 1958).

self, Emmet took over the end of the play and I felt I had to let him.[99]

Perhaps Johnston's wavering here accounts for this peculiar legend: the representatives of the Irish Republican Army, sent to the second performance of the opening run with instructions to close down the show if it proved uncongenial to their ideals, left well satisfied that *The Old Lady* could pass their muster.[100]

Insistence on the play's visionary possibilities depends on the moment of the play when the Speaker finally understands the nature of his prophetic role, and recites his apostrophe to Dublin. Here at last he accepts the other face of Sarah, the harridan aspect of the "Old Mother," previously a cause of horror. At the beginning of his nightmare, the Speaker had experienced a vision of "deadbosom" Sarah. A horde of indistinguishable Irish forms, a "brood of sorry scuts," curse their reviled mother in a variety of ways during the course of the play — a pyschological trick common in Irish literature and one that circumvents the need for social and political praxis. In the apostrophe, the Speaker says they curse her even as they "break from the womb." The images of birth and suckling at the end of the play resonate with the earlier images of female fecundity and failed motherhood. But at the close of the play, following the crooked road of fools, the Speaker sees his Old Mother, "the Strumpet City," walking the streets of Paradise "Head high and unashamed."

In the first version of the play where these complex issues are more transparent, the Speaker had proclaimed:

The world is very weak and wan and sad
But I myself have made her as she is
And prize her as she is, until I make
A newer and a better world to bear the
flame of my desire.[101]

If the arrogant young man here arrogates to himself the power to create and shape a material/female world, he now at least also accepts responsibility for the failures of the past. In other words, one cannot awake from the nightmare of history

99. Interview with Christine St. Peter, 8 March 1976, Toronto.

100. *Record*, 227–28. The account in Johnston's diary entry appears as well in a *Sunday Dispatch* (8 July 1932) review of the 1932 Cape edition.

101. *Alpha*, Leaf 70.

unless one can carry that history, transformed, into the future. The Speaker's awakening is the beginning of action. With this decision he can make Ireland one of the nations of the earth.

In all versions of the play Johnston had great difficulty balancing these elements and rewrote the end of the play again and again in an effort to hit the right note of ambiguity—that refusal to tell his audience what side of the fence they should be sitting on. In order to evaluate his achievement here and elsewhere in the play, we need to examine some of the important revisions he made to the play over a fifty-year period.

IV. READING THE TEXTUAL HISTORY

The Old Lady Says "No!" had a history of composition that extended over half a century. Always eager to resist mental and artistic "positions," Johnston revised his work whenever a new production or chance of publication made revision possible. And because *The Old Lady* is a play that remains socially and politically topical, he needed to change a number of details from time to time to maintain the experience of contemporaneity. Add to these changes two false starts, each a full-length version of the play, and we find over two hundred pages of revisions.

Eight extant versions of the play remain. Johnston very carefully preserved and retrospectively classified the different versions of his works, so the stages of composition can be charted quite precisely. The primary papers related to this play he gathered under the title *Uranus,* the first "planet" in his literary cosmogony.

The first three complete versions are unpublished typescripts. These he later called *Uranus Alpha, Uranus Beta,* and *Uranus Delta.* The *Gamma* that should logically follow *Beta* appears to exist, in reference only, on the title page of *Beta*; here Johnston wrote that the corrections made on that typescript were "Corrections for *Gamma.*" These corrections are virtually identical to the *Delta* text.

Alpha, the first version, is a two-act play consisting of seventy-two typewritten leaves. This script is lightly annotated by an unidentified hand, with comments that primarily criticize the play's length. There is also a file of eighty-five leaves called "Alpha Odd Sheets"; these, combined with *Alpha,* provide the corrections for *Beta.*

The *Beta* typescript, with only one act and fifty-four leaves, was read closely by Yeats, who objected strenuously to what he read. He crossed out 260 lines of the *Beta* version, almost a tenth of the total play, as well as questioning other passages. Occasionally he even offered a possible alteration. Johnston later wrote "as finally rejected" on the title page of this version.[102] All the marginal revisions on this typescript appear in the *Delta* version.

Delta has two acts and sixty-nine leaves, nearly the original length, and is almost certainly the *Rhapsody in Green* version he referred to in his diary entry.[103] This typescript served as the Gate Theatre prompt copy, and has technical instructions written in the margins: perfunctory lighting instructions, the cast list, a list of expenses,[104] and what appear to be markings for rehearsal blocks.

Two other unpublished versions of the play exist. One is a script adapted by Johnston for radio, performed on Radio Eireann on 23 October 1955. The other is a television script prepared without Johnston's help and, according to his own judgment, not properly part of the play's textual history. This version, directed by Michael Leesto-Smith, was performed on BBC television 13 March 1964.[105]

The other three versions of the play are published. The first, virtually the same as *Delta*, was published in 1932 by Jonathan Cape of London. The second, slightly revised, appeared in 1960 from Jonathan Cape, and in the same form and year by Little, Brown in Boston. The definitive version, according to Johnston, was published in 1977 by Colin Smythe, Ltd., and serves as the copy text for this edition.

Predating these versions there exists a fascinating record

---

102. The typescripts' title pages have been mixed around; *Alpha*'s is on *Beta*, *Beta*'s is among a sheaf of 85 "odd sheets for *Alpha*" with the typescripts. It seems impossible to determine *Delta*'s original title. These papers are at Trinity College, with the exception of *Beta*, sold by Johnston in 1965 to the University of Victoria (Canada) Special Collections.

103. *Record* 8, p. 201.

104. Hilton Edward's salary, £100; staff salaries, £20; [salaries? for actresses] Susan Hunt, Sheila Carey, and Pauline Besson, a total of £50; Art. O'Murnaghan, £5; [?], £6; Ida Moore, £4; [?], £[?]; lights, £100; costumes, £70; sets, £30; properties, £25; teas, £20; music, £50.

105. The BBC director made basic errors in interpretation, most obviously the casting of two actresses for Sarah Curran and the Old Flower Woman, when the play demands one actress capable of playing the two manifestations of the same woman.

of Johnston's first plans for this play. While Johnston was qualifying in 1925 for the Bar in England, he began jotting down ideas for his first play in a notebook half filled with practice answers to questions on Constitutional Law. Twenty-four pages of the notebook, 419 lines, are devoted to ideas for the play: bits of dialogue; lists of possible characters; an historical bibliography; an outline for scenes; snippets of advice to himself about how to write the play; and, perhaps most useful, cryptic but straightforward explanations of his intentions for the play. The notebook's contents are disorganized and tentative—he was apparently thinking out ideas as he wrote—and possibly written over a period of time.

He was not concerned in the notebook, or later, with building "characters": instead he was illustrating an idea or presenting an institution or class of people by giving them lines meant to be representative of a state of mind. Thus he projected not one statue but several who would dispute differing concepts of Irish nationalism. George III complains that "all the Irish are the same. Half of them serve a foreign king and insist on religious independence. The rest of them want an Irish Republic but go to Rome for their salvation." The "sentimental pro-Irish Englishman," Admiral Nelson, complains, too: "Why can't you [Irish] sit still and enjoy your romantic country?" Grattan responds that "romance is an escape from crude reality. A cheap drug." To which the nineteenth-century Irish poet Thomas Moore cries: "No, it is a real creative force Appassionata, the will to reach the yet to be. What we will, will be. (The women know that)." Johnston struck out Moore's name, then noted that these are not "real characters but warring sentiments in the Auditor's mind."[106]

This treatment of voices shows the influence of the German expressionist drama, where a central figure moves not from scene to scene but from station to station, at each one meeting types of people speaking in illustrative epigrams. According to the notebook, the Speaker will visit six stations, each a significant locus of Dublin life, and at each he will think momentarily that he has reached Rathfarnham, his particular Land of Heart's Desire. This search will culminate in the "execution scene" that ends the play, and the "metamorphosis of

---

106. The "Speaker" was called the "Auditor" only in the notebook.

29

the slum." The only station that Johnston labelled expressionist in this notebook was that of Grafton Street, Dublin's fashionable shopping street where he gathered wealthy Dublin Protestants or "West Britons" to exchange tag lines by way of conversation.

From Grafton Street the notebook would have Emmet stumble into the Abbey Theatre, where a "Macardle drama" is playing: "The Abbey is acting an Irish Patriotic Play and doing it badly. / You can tell that they are acting." This became the opening playlet in the finished play, and these stage directions demonstrate that from the first Johnston intended the satire. Moreover, his target was specific: Dorothy Macardle, as a playwright and nationalist historian, had three plays presented at the Abbey between 1918 and 1925, and her *Ann Kavanagh,* produced in April 1922, opened with the song "The Shan Van Vocht," an evocative touch Johnston stole for his own overture.

One of the stations projected in the notebook is the Dáil, the lower house of the Irish Parliament. The primary point of attack here is the offensive clubbiness: "Coldness of impersonal officialdom. Warmth when a personal relation is established, and it is discovered he is a Cork man. . . . Can't get him in as a visitor, so gets him in as a member." The Dáil, only fourteen lines in the notebook, expands into sixteen of *Alpha*'s seventy-two leaves. But after Lennox Robinson suggested cutting the scene from the *Alpha* version, Johnston never used any part of it again, preferring to focus on daily lives instead of official institutions.

The Salon scene, crucial in all versions of the play, is not included among the original stations in the notebook, although Johnston devoted three pages there to sketching choral and antiphonal voices later used at the party. The sketchy dialogue below indicates how Johnston would satirize the values and behavior of the middle-class Free State leaders—conservative, jingoistic, and philistine:

VOICES I love music—so clever. . . . Celebrity Concerts. Don't you love Wagner. . . . Shelley—Keats—Yeats. "We always have some of the best statues round on Sunday evenings for a little music." Gunman General introduced under many names. "May Auditor sing?" "Has he a good record in the National Movement?" "Where was he in

Easter Week?"[107] "Smith. That doesn't sound very Irish. It does when you call it O'Smidda."

Johnston devoted a quarter of his notebook to dialogue for the statues. Their reduction to one in the play parallels another reduction that must have cost Johnston much more. These are the Shadows who appear in the penultimate scene of the play and whose appearance supplies the original title of the play, *Shadowdance*. They are to quote lines from great Irish authors whom Johnston later called "some of Dublin's greatest contributors to the World's Knowledge of itself."[108] These shadows were meant to dispel the gaseous vapors of Dublin speech, and to prepare the audience for Emmet's closing address. Like the Speaker, they will be mocked by the Dublin "forms," and, like him, they will persist in delivering their prophetic lines. In the notebook Johnston listed thirteen authors for inclusion: Sean O'Casey, G. B. Shaw, Oscar Wilde, W. B. Yeats, Richard Sheridan, John Millington Synge, James Clarence Mangan, Thomas Moore, AE, Padraic Colum, Oliver Goldsmith, James Joyce, and Charles Lever. Jonathan Swift makes an appearance in later versions, but by the 1977 edition only four shadows remain: Yeats, Joyce, Wilde, and Shaw. While these may represent Johnston's personal pantheon of Irish writers, the reduction was due to structural demands; Johnston feared tiring his audience with "the interminable ending."[109]

Perhaps the most significant entry in the notebook is the specific explanation of the Auditor's vision: "'I will create the substance of my dream. I have been carried along too long. . . . Thence via mock Rathfarnham to the Slum where the Blind Man orates on the folly of dreams. . . . Auditor marches crisis by crisis to his ebb tide in the slum. There he triumphs over adversity and the perversity of his fellows by creative genius. The metamorphosis of the slum." At the notebook stage of the play's development, the visionary victory is the primary focus. This will change as the years proceed.

Between the notebook and *Alpha*, Johnston performed that inexplicable alchemy whereby a collection of ideas becomes a coherent play. But the development from *Alpha* to *Delta* is

---

107. It became a matter of some importance in subsequent Irish politics to be able to claim participation in the nationalist ranks during the Easter Rising of 1916.

108. "A Note on What Happened," p. 130.

109. Letter to Christine St. Peter, 3 June 1977, Dalkey, Ireland.

equally striking. These typescripts indirectly present a record of the clash between Yeats and Johnston; they also reveal the young dramatist disciplining his bludgeoning first attempt into the effective art of a mature playwright.

In the discussion of the texts that follows, there is no attempt to include all revisions; I include only those that might contribute to the interpretation of the final play. The synoptic chart clarifies the relationships among the versions. Significant revisions within the scenes will be elaborated below.

Synoptic Chart

ALPHA	BETA	DELTA
Act One	*One Act Only*	*Act One*
Playlet	[similar]	[similar]
Doctor on stage	[similar]	[similar]
Dublin "forms"	[similar]	[similar]
Dublin street	[similar]	[similar]
———	———	Emmet and stage hand
Emmet, Grattan, and the Old Lady	[similar]	[similar]
Blind Man	[similar]	[similar]
Grafton Street	[similar]	[similar]
Dáil scene	Phibs' girls	[similar]
———	———	Crowd scene and trial
Emmet shoots Joe	———	Emmet shoots Joe
Act Two		*Act Two*
Tea Party	[similar]	[similar]
Emmet, Blind Man	[similar]	[similar]
Andy	———	———
Dublin lovers	[similar]	[similar]
Emmet and Sarah	[similar]	[similar]
Tenement scene	[similar]	[similar]
Shadowdance	[similar]	[similar]
Dock speech	[similar]	[similar]
———	———	Doctor returns

All versions of the play open with a short love scene minutes before Emmet's arrest. In *Alpha* and *Beta* this little scene opens with Sarah, alone, calling out from her window towards the mountain Kilmashogue: "Blue mountains / Tibradden, purple robed in the silver moonlight / My own wild whispering Kilkakee / Guard and keep my love from harm. / White roadway / Wandering ribbon roadway / Bring my lover back to me.

[She starts] Who is there? / I heard a rustling in the trees! / Who is there, I say?"

For *Delta,* Johnston replaced this poetic passage of his own creation with Mangan's "Fair Hills of Eire" and Darley's "Serenade of a Loyal Martyr." Henceforth there would be no mistaking the intention of the ornate writing. But in *Alpha* and *Beta* the florid writing continues. Robert Emmet, the Speaker, makes his appearance:

> SPEAKER [*with appropriate gesture*] Hush, beloved. It is I.
>
> SARAH Robert! You! Where are you, my dear?
>
> SPEAKER Sally, my loved one!
>
> SARAH Oh Robert, Robert, why have you ventured down? You are in danger. The soldiers are everywhere.
>
> SPEAKER The soldiers! Have they been searching for me here?
>
> SARAH Last night they ransacked the house. They even broke into my boudoir.
>
> SPEAKER [*his eyes blazing*] God!

When Sarah urges Robert to go, Robert is given the opportunity to proclaim his dream of leading Ireland into revolution. Of the forty-seven lines this takes, here are representative samples. (The bracketed parts indicate Yeats's deletions.)

> SPEAKER How can I fly? Where can I fly? / [The mountains are full of a wild singing, / and the streets are throbbing with the / rush of feet and the crying of angry voices.] I have lit such a flame in my / heart that all the waters of the Erne / could never quench, a flame that burns and / tortures me with everlasting anguish. . . .

Urged by Sarah to save himself, Robert declares his passionate readiness to dare "all for Ireland and all again for Sarah Curran" because it is "a glorious thing to dare." When Sarah too sensibly replies that "it is a terrible thing to die," Robert is given his great chance:

> SPEAKER To die? Do you think that I can be afraid / to die? [I, the poor hunted fox: broken, / driven to the hills, lying panting in the / bracken and stealing out only when night / creeps down from the east to cloak my / nakedness.]

> But I have unfurled the green / flag in the streets. I have cried aloud / [from the high places to the peoples

of / the earth,] "The Gael still lives!" / "The Gael is still unconquered and / undying!" I have [put on the uniform of my country and] drawn the sword . . . to strike / a blow against the stranger. "I have / written [my name in letters of fire] across / the page of history." "The Key to Liberty / is the Sword"! ["The Sword must be kept / clean and bright!"] Ah, do you think that / I can be afraid to die?

Since Yeats thought the speeches were sincerely intended, his deletions made good sense. But Yeats also tried to repair the deliberately fulsome language as well: for example, Johnston's thirty-one-word "poor hunted fox" sentence became, in Yeats's revision, the simple "I am as homeless as a fox."

The lovers' scene is interrupted by the arrival of the British troops led by Major Sirr. In *Alpha/Beta*, the arresting officer has the broad characterization of a villain of melodrama:

SIRR Hah! What fools! They make it too easy for us. . . . All we have to do is to put a watch upon his Mistress and within two days he walks into the trap.

SPEAKER This is too much! Take back that word! Take back that word!

SIRR (with a laugh) A pretty wench, too. Not that she'll be lonely long, I'll warrant. . . .

Although Yeats left Sirr alone, Johnston dignified him for *Delta*, perhaps to protect the authority of Grattan's statue with whom Sirr doubles. But the lovers fare less well after *Beta*. Their lines are reduced to an exchange of lines of poetry torn from their contexts and patched together so pertinently that they almost, but never quite, make sense. Even to an audience that did not grow up memorizing the kinds of romantic-patriotic poems assembled in the *Dublin Book of Irish Verse* from which Johnston adopted these lines, the playlet is unmistakably satiric.[110]

The stage business ensuing from the concussion to the Speaker that ends the playlet and throws him into the nightmare of modern Dublin remains essentially unchanged throughout all versions. So does the superbly effective concatenation in

110. Ed. John Cooke (Dublin: Hodges, Figgis and Co., 1909). Johnston chose these poems because "everyone in Dublin knew them all by heart." Interview with Christine St. Peter, 8 March 1976, Toronto.

the street with its alien *umwelt* so characteristic of expressionist theatre and films. In *Alpha* and *Beta*, the Speaker moves to his encounter with the old flower woman and Grattan's statue, which still stands with upstretched arm facing Trinity College, where Robert Emmet had been a student. Since this is just at the foot of Grafton Street, Johnston was moving his action with the topographical care of James Joyce's *Ulysses*, a copy of which Johnston owned by 1926.[111] Even the beggar has been a typical feature in this landscape, so Johnston's use of her here as avatar of Old Mother Dublin and Cathleen ni Houlihan is a savage comment on Dublin's social and economic realities. In *Delta*, the action between Emmet and the Stage Hand precedes the Grattan exchange, a device that underscores the artificiality of the theatrical illusion. And since the stage hand transmogrifies into the Minister of Arts and Crafts in act 2 of *Delta*, Johnston deftly drew Irish politics, language, and art into the realm of play-acting.

Alpha particularly exploits the metaphor of Irish politics as theatre in the Dáil scene that fills most of act 1. After his humiliating defeat by Grattan's statue, the Speaker is plunged into the Irish Parliament, where he unsuccessfully pleads his cause among Ireland's real actors—the politicians and journalists. Since the Dáil had met for the first time in 1919, this scene was acutely topical at the time of its composition in 1926. But it was nearly a quarter of *Alpha* and the most derivative of Johnston's attempts.

It is only in the Dáil scene, which disappears completely after *Beta*, that we can find significant traces of the influence Johnston claimed in his "Opus One": George S. Kaufman and Marc Connelly's *Beggar on Horseback* (1925). Johnston's humorous scene and the American comedy use extravagantly inflated expressionist devices as a way of satirizing the respective national characters. Both focus on the way journalists irresponsibly create events as a way of fueling their perennial need for news. In each play the inflamed hero commits a murder for which society-at-large condemns him.[112]

The Dáil scene opens with a loud voice announcing that a

---

111. *3rd Omnibus*, 16 May 1926, p. 52.
112. This element occurs as well in Ernst Toller's *Hopplà*, but without the humor.

strike is still on "in here." Desperate to escape from the street and the taunts of Grattan's statue, Emmet seeks entry. In an extended comic routine, the Military Policeman does not recognize Robert Emmet's name or costume; he finally gains admission when he admits to being a relation of Paddy Emmet of Clonakilty. The following stage directions give a good sense of the tone and action of the entire Dáil episode:

> The curtains fade from [the Speaker's] grasp and part showing something suggestive of the Dáil. Fuss and movement. Attendants with Programmes and bundles of correspondence pass to and fro. In the centre of the front bench sits the Old Flower Woman. Two fantastic Newspaper Men with notebooks and small megaphones chat in the foreground. A distant subdued roaring like the shouting of many voices can be heard. Sometimes during the action it almost dies away but it seldom quite ceases. As the Speaker walks in, there is a heavy clapping of hands.

The Dáil atmosphere quickly metamorphoses into a sporting event with attendants selling programs for the "Match." Urged by the newsmen to speak, the Speaker resumes his playlet lines but after two pages of floundering and amidst general inattention, he is finally interrupted by a Minister's challenge: "What we want to know is this; what is the Deputy's position? Is he prepared to support the Government upon the question of Schedule B?"

Mention of Schedule B provokes hot debate among the Members, all eagerly reported in distorting headlines through the newmen's megaphones. When all discover that Emmet has no position on Schedule B and that, moveover, he is wearing carpet slippers, a vociferous debate develops: Can the Dáil suspend "Order 10, Subsection 5 of the Standing Orders of Dáil Eireann" that states: "No Deputy shall stand about in carpet slippers?" These carpet slippers remain a crucial element in all versions, the deflationary device that marks the way clothes make the hero.

A nationalist, a labor member, and a rural politican strike characteristic rhetorical poses in an ever noisier debate, which the journalists report as the start of a "DARING OUTRAGE." When two soldiers casually stroll in, their arrival signals "MILITARY ON THE MOVE." The Speaker, now thoroughly befuddled, wants to enlist:

SPEAKER I've come to join up. The country wants men!

1ST SOLDIER What for?

SPEAKER Why . . . to put a stop to all this . . . to fight. . . . This trouble . . . don't you know. It's all about me really. I must join in. I want a gun.

1ST SOLDIER Well, come back in the morning some time.

With the "military" the only calm ones, the Speaker becomes wild; seizing a gun he fires into the darkness. In the silence that follows they discover he has shot a man.

When Johnston removed the Dáil scene, he needed another transition from the expressionism of Grafton Street to the Tea Party. He managed this by expanding the number of speakers on Grafton Street, an addition Yeats disliked, but Johnston maintained. The Flapper and Trinity Medical student are joined by older versions of themselves, a Business Man and a Well-dressed Woman, all these of Johnston's own social class.[113]

But the crucial additions to the Grafton Street voices are those of Katie and Lizzie (Bernadette and Carmel in the 1977 edition). These Johnston calls the "two young things" from Phibsborough, a working-class neighborhood in north Dublin. For help in writing these unfamiliar voices he appealed to his friend Kate Curling, an Abbey Theatre actress. She wrote him a letter full of the locutions and recreations of the Phibs' Girls.[114] In *Beta* Katie turns up as the maid in the home where the tea party is being held, so she ushers in Emmet and the new scene. In *Delta* and subsequent versions, the greatly expanded dialogue of the "Phibs' Girls" performs added functions. They furnish another class's version of Dublin's tawdry courting conventions; and they provoke the crisis that results in the crowd scene and Emmet's public trial when they accuse him of sexual assault.

The voices of Grafton Street are meant to utter the most current banalities. For this reason, at each new publication Johnston attempted to change somewhat the details that were no longer topical. Trams became buses; Elizabeth Arden, not the

---

113. For the Woman's lines, Johnston just copied the mail from his mother's desk. Interview with Christine St. Peter, 24 June 1977, Dalkey.

114. This letter is among Johnston's papers at Trinity College.

Boncilla Method, replaced drooping tissue; a baby Austin gave way to a yellow M.G.; the Trinity Dramatic changed to the Trinity Players; the young folk frequent the Dewdrop Inn instead of Fuller's Confectionary shop. Since all these details are intentionally of the most fleeting sort, it was impossible to keep them current, and Johnston attempted to do so only half-heartedly. For example, although he changed the name of Dingle's Band to the Wet Dreams for the 1977 edition, he never bothered to replace the dated reference to the song "Tea for Two." Some names were thematically too relevant to relinquish, like the nail polish called "Heart's Despair."

The difference between the Dáil scene and the crowd/trial scene of post-*Beta* versions reveals most clearly Johnston's growing skill. While the Dáil scene is very amusing, it has the slapstick quality of a vaudeville routine, and tends to blame the news media exclusively for the hysteria of Emmet's revolutionary actions. The crowd scene that Johnston worked out for *Delta* is far subtler in its analysis of mob psychology. For this version Johnston chose a richer inspiration: instead of the frothy Broadway play *Beggar on Horseback,* he borrowed from a local exemplar, Joyce's *Ulysses.*[115] The crowd scene is strikingly reminiscent of the dramatic *Circe* episode; like Leopold Bloom, the Speaker is forced to defend his vision, which he accomplishes so successfully that he inspires his listeners to follow him to Curran's Cross and the New Jerusalem (Joyce's "new Bloomusalem in the Nova Hibernia of the future"). Like Leopold Bloom, however, he loses his followers; he fails to "justify" himself to the citizens' "court."

But here as elsewhere Johnston transformed his source to fit his own purposes. In *Circe,* Bloom is accused of being as "bad as Parnell was"; Johnston's Emmet, the self-appointed savior, proclaims himself a new Parnell with the boast: "Until this party deposes me I am leader." This reference to the brilliant but controversial Irish parliamentarian (1846–91) allowed Johnston to initiate two important leitmotifs: the mutual betrayal of the Irish and their leaders; and the sexual puritanism/prurience that corrupts their perceptions and relationships. The crowd sniffs sexual transgression ("abattoir of licentiousness") where

---

115. Vivian Mercier pointed out this influence as early as 1948: "Perfection of the Life," in *Denis Johnston: A Retrospective,* pp. 231–32.

none exists, and the Speaker consummates his passion not with sex but with gunfire.

Johnston emphasized this latter motif by including in *Delta* extensive allusions to another of his major sources: Yeats's *Cathleen ni Houlihan*. In that play, as in *The Old Lady*, Cathleen declares that "it is not food and drink I want. . . . It is not silver I want." When pressed, Yeats's Cathleen says, "If anyone would give me help he must give me himself, he must give me all." But hers is a chaste demand: "With all the lovers that brought me their love I never set out bed for any." Johnston's Old Lady, daughter of Houlihan and of Mike Magilligan,[116] mixes her call for young men's blood with a lewder request, an innuendo that becomes sexual solicitation in the tenement scene of act 2.

In *Delta*, this crowd sequence had begun with Grattan's statue, symbol of reason and legality, being entrapped in the folds of the black curtains. The curtains, representing layers of the Speaker's consciousness, thus blot out the principle of order that might have prevented the Speaker's nightmare. In this version only, Johnston represented this absence by leaving Grattan's pedestal visible but empty during the scene. As the act closes, the Old Woman mounts the pedestal and delivers these lines from Yeats's *Cathleen*: "Do not make great keening / When the graves have been dug tomorrow. / Do not call the white-scarfed riders / To the burying. . . ." In the subsequent, published versions of his play, Johnston eliminated the Old Woman's symbolic ascent. In doing so he lost a powerful visual image but also prevented a facile opposition between Grattan/Order and the Old Woman/Disorder. By the end of act 2 the Speaker and audience will have to learn to see disorder in order and all the Old Woman's aspects as "redeemable."

Johnston left almost untouched the original Tea Party, although in his 1977 Abbey Programme Notes he explained that he thought this whole scene should be redone in the modern vernacular of the television talk, the perfect milieu for "my Emmet and his Sarah Ní Hooligan."

The satiric clarity of the Tea Party is not matched in the

---

116. One of Johnston's favorite bar-room songs, "Mike Magilligan's Daughter, Mary Anne," combines in *Delta* with the final words of Yeats's play: "Oh, she doesn't paint nor powdher / An her figger-is-all-her-owin. / Hoopsie-daisie! The walk of a Quee-in!"

following scene, where Emmet meets the Blind Man. In part we are confused by the parodic use of Synge's dialect. Gene A. Barnett, for example, sees the Blind Man as a symbol of "heroic Ireland gone to unhealthy seed, a blind maker of jigs and tunes who must live on the remains of the dead past."[117] But in 1977 Johnston considered his a voice of reason similar to Grattan's.[118] An examination of the typescript revisions shows how this ambiguity developed, and how much Johnston probably forgot about his earlier inspirations.

In *Alpha* the Blind Man is a ridiculous figure, reminiscent of Martin Doul in Synge's *The Well of the Saints*. He extravagantly admires a night watchman named Andy, who has convinced him that he is the "King of Terenure" and a descendent of the heroic kings of Thomond. *Alpha*'s Blind Man is a gull; by *Beta* he has incorporated Andy's conning tricks and can feel out the would-be hero, whom he scolds for keeping alive "in lazy, idle hearts" the memory of the "dead, the half dead and them that will never die."

In the midst of their discussion, a "He" and a "She" appear, an older and more cynical version of the Flapper and Medical Student. With Andy, the Blind Man, and Emmet, we eavesdrop on the abortive courting ritual; it is a superb psychological study in its *Alpha* form but, with the Andy material, covers twelve leaves of typescript. Johnston dramatically shortened their scene and eliminated Andy altogether in the much more economical *Beta*, then maintained these cuts in *Delta* and subsequent versions. In doing so, however, he conflated the qualities previously distributed between Andy and the Blind Man. So the Blind Man must combine, somewhat incongruously, a strong connection with the kingdom of the Dead and the wisdom to condemn Dublin for being "No City of the Living: but of the Dark and the Dead!"

Johnston needed the Blind Man to summon up the shadows of Ireland's great writers for the shadowdance. But first he had to establish that moment when the world of the living and the dead intersect: for this he moved to the tenement scene where we witness the death of Joe, the man shot by Emmet in act 1.

Emmet had been frightened by the Blind Man's vision of

117. Barnett, 36.
118. Letter to Christine St. Peter, 3 June 1977, Dalkey.

Dubliners inhabited by literary and historical *incubi*, especially as he was told he was one of them. As happens in all versions of the play, in moments of Emmet's panic the lights go off and, once again, he hears Sarah Curran summoning him. As in act 1, when the lights come on he finds himself with that other aspect of Sarah, the Old Flower Woman, but this time in her tenement home and with three men who are, at least symbolically, her sons.

Each man reveals a different shade of revolutionary Ireland: the fiery young "diehard"; the older man for whom "Free State" means open pubs; and the dying patriot poet, Joe, who lies on his deathbed composing poems. In Joe, Johnston was probably satirizing the "three bad poets" of the 1916 Rising: Patrick Pearse, Joseph Mary Plunkett, and Thomas MacDonagh, whose poetry combined with their Republicanism as necessary co-stimulants.[119] He was also parodying act 2 of O'Casey's *The Plough and the Stars*. Everyone in the tenement room is inebriated with something—alcohol, political vision, the desire for money or for sex, sentimental poetry, or some combination of these. In *Beta* only, Emmet later calls these men the "Shouters, the Swillers and the Scribblers on the wall" and declares, ambiguously, that he has learned a lesson from them.

In *Alpha* and *Beta* Joe recites lines, just before he dies, that had been assigned to the Speaker in the Notebook. Yeats wanted all the lines in brackets deleted:

[To-morrow night]
[I'll sit astride the moon]
[And play the devil with the baby stars.]
[To-morrow night!]
Ah, God is good!
And Death forever dead
[For He has fashioned an eternal Morrow]

In *Delta* Johnston substituted for the whole speech a humorously melodramatic farewell from Joe that remains in all subsequent versions. But in the revisons made in *Beta*'s margins, Johnston added, after Joe's death, lines for the Speaker that are arguably the most important in the play:

---

119. Peter Costello (*The Heart Grown Brutal*, [Dublin: Gill and Macmillan, 1977], 73–90) discusses, somewhat contentiously, the cross-fertilization of literature and revolution.

Can I change all this then? Must I? What is the meaning of it all?

This speech changes slightly in *Delta* and the 1932 Cape edition:

Gone. A bloody playactor. Am I then to alter this for myself? By myself?

And in the 1960 Cape and 1977 Smythe version:

Gone. And I am only a play actor—unless I dare to contradict the dead! Must I do that?

These slight modifications demonstrate the characteristic pains Johnston took in working over his earlier versions. Sometimes the revisions add little, but in this case, each change is a clarification of the Speaker's prophetic role.

Before the Speaker orates, the Dubliners come to pay respects to a man they honor in death but whom they culpably neglected to notice when alive. Joe passes "into the ranks of the Government" in a display of what Johnston called the "immediate and grotesque idealization of whoever has died, however unworthy."[120] And in case we should miss the point, Johnston added in *Delta* yet another swipe at Yeats's *Cathleen* with Lady Trimmer's unctious: "So yellow-haired Donough [sic] is dead! Dear, dear!" But even Grattan's statue is not immune to the drama of death. In *Alpha* his only comment is: "Death, creeping like a mist at the heels of my countrymen! It is all we are good for." In the *Delta*–1977 Smythe versions Johnston allowed Grattan's statue to relent somewhat, perhaps to illustrate that even the rational succumb to such moments: "A word-spinner dying gracefully with a text upon his lips. The symbol of Ireland's genius. Never mind. He died well. He knew how to do that."

The Speaker suddenly disappears during this scene, as he too passes into the land of the Dead, whence he will return as one of the Irish Shadows—a touch that elevates his author into the ranks of the shadowdancers. Yeats did not like Johnston's use of indistinct forms behind gauze curtains in the Shadowdance and wanted him to use instead "recognisable forms."[121] But Johnston maintained his original presentation: disembodied words had a life of their own and he would have the right

---

120. Interview with Christine St. Peter, 8 March 1976, Toronto.

121. Yeats did not, however, correct Johnston's misquotation of his poem "Into the Twilight."

sort of language assuming preeminence among his audiences, one on the stage, one in the auditorium proper.

The speeches Johnston devised in *Alpha* and *Beta* for Emmet's dock speech are so florid and clumsy that it is difficult to believe that he intended anything other than satire. Yet this appears not to be the case. In the playlet, when he intended satire he accentuated the ridiculous in revision. In the dock speech, his method of revision for *Delta* consisted of patching together allusions to works he unquestionably admired. Here is a passage from *Beta* characteristic of the three-page peroration Emmet delivers:

> It is easier to laugh than to be wise. Better to shake your sides than wring your hearts. So laugh away. I am content. You think that I am mad. I know, because I see it in your faces. I sense it in the measure of your covert glance from eye to eye. But, O my friends, think well before you fling that berserk boomerang about this giddy globe. You think I am a fool, and you are right—a moonstruck, vain, inefficacious fool, that dared to tilt against the wisdom of the ages, and batter on the bars of incommutable Reality —a fool that was betrayed, as always fools must be. But, O my friends, let mercy mingle with your merriment, for what one of us can tell when he derides the feeble folly of a poor romanticist that he is not flogging the carcase of his own dead heart? Might not I, like you, run to take refuge with the cowards and the weary of heart and those of little faith in that sanctuary for broken dreamers which the world calls "cynicism" . . . ?

A bit of this and Johnston had his stage audience laugh, shuffle about, or applaud. Yeats was less agreeable: alongside the passage above he wrote "rubbish," then the withering comment that "cynicism was a worn out commonplace thirty years ago." But Johnston's Speaker had continued for another two pages. After Yeats's dismissal, Johnston abandoned his own invention, driven to the not uncommon twentieth-century expedient of creating poetic language by borrowing from earlier poets. A decade later Johnston commented somewhat ruefully on this method:

> [*The Old Lady Says "No!"*] is a spontaneous reaction, following an age of false, romantic values and rancid political clichés, and it was bound to have been written by some-

body. But what a pity it was not written by a Poet instead of a Half-Coherent who, whenever he finds himself staggered by the gigantic issues he has raised, has nothing better to do than to fall back upon Dante and Holy Writ! It is true that these issues are fundamentally religious ones, but what they cry out for is to be restated in the language of great verse, rather than in that of a revivalist meeting.[122]

But if Johnston felt this a personal failure, it produced the happy effect of allowing him to lift his play out of its parochial Dublin setting and onto the stage of European religion and literature. The romance, at first the search for Rathfarnham, quickly expands into as universal a quest as Johnston could manage. He built into the Emmet figure echoes of Don Quixote tilting against the "wisdom of the ages"; William Blake navigating through the worlds of innocence and experience; Ulysses in pursuit of Ithaca/Penelope; the wandering Jew longing for Jerusalem; Macbeth fighting for a kingdom; Galahad on the quest for the Holy Grail; Leopold Bloom travelling toward his Molly; Dante caught in the dark wood in his journey toward Paradise; and, finally, Christ harrowing hell.

The "Strumpet City" apostrophe appears in all versions and with only very minor changes, although in *Alpha* and *Beta* Johnston had blurred its rhetorical effect by adding another long passage in which Emmet talks to Sarah. Here is *Beta*'s curtain speech (the ellipses are Johnston's):

> I am so tired, Sally . . . but I am happy . . . happy because of you and of the infinite goodness of God. I am going to sleep, perhaps for quite a long time . . . But never mind. I will be dreaming that I am still down there, awake and walking through the streets . . . with my arm around your dear waist and your head resting on my shoulder . . . starved, tortuous streets . . . festering streets . . . But the children are laughing, dear . . . the children . . . are . . . laughing. . . .

Stage directions after this anti-climactic sentimentality have the Speaker go to sleep/death while "two dim figures, a man and a girl, his arm around her waist, presently pass slowly across behind the gauze curtain." In *Delta*, however, the revised directions remind the audience of the theatrical artifice of the entire

---

122. "Drama: Drama and Belfast," *Bell* 3:5 (February 1942), 359–60.

play. Johnston eliminated the couple and reintroduced the doctor whose earlier departure from the stage had begun the dream play. He "places one finger to his lips, and makes a sign for the front curtains to be drawn" while he covers the prostrate Speaker.

In the 1977 Smythe edition Johnston changed this ending once again. Here he allowed the doctor to finish the sentence that began the dream at the play's beginning, "that will. . . ." The added words are ". . . do, fine." This should jolt the audience firmly from the world of the Speaker's dream. But the words also assent, if slightly ironically, to the Speaker's final words: "There now. Let my epitaph be written."

A NOTE ON THE TEXT

This edition uses the version of the play as finally emended by Denis Johnston for publication in 1977 by Colin Smythe, Ltd. The changes the author made for that version erase some of the original 1920s flavor found in the play's first edition published in 1932 by Jonathan Cape, Ltd. They do, however, represent the culmination of a fifty-year process of revision to a play the author wished to keep contemporary, since the conditions dramatized in the play he believed still current in Ireland.

I have silently corrected the Irish words that Johnston tended to misspell. Words in the Irish language (but not words of Irish derivation that have become part of the Hibernian-English dialect of Ireland) are italicized.

BIBLIOGRAPHY

PRIMARY WORKS

Denis Johnston. "The Making of the Theatre." In *The Gate Theatre: Dublin*. Ed. Bulmer Hobson. Dublin: The Gate Theatre, 1934.

————. *Record: 1924–32*. Trinity College Library.

————. *3rd Omnibus: 1924–1934*. Trinity College Library.

INTERVIEWS AND CORRESPONDENCE

Denis Johnston. *"An Interview with Denis Johnston."* with Gordon Henderson. *Journal of Irish Literature* 2 (May–September 1973): 2–3.

Personal interviews with Christine St. Peter. 8 March 1976, Toronto; 7–12 and 15–24 July 1976, Dalkey, Ireland.

Letters to Christine St. Peter. 8 June 1976, 3 June 1977, 12 March 1978.

PARTIAL CRITICAL BIBLIOGRAPHY

Barrett, Gene A. *Denis Johnston*. Boston: Twayne, 1978.

Canfield, Curtis. *Plays of Changing Ireland*. New York: Macmillan, 1936.

Edwards, Hilton. *The Mantle of Harlequin*. Dublin: Progress House, 1958.

Ferrar, Harold. *Denis Johnston's Irish Theatre*. Dublin: Dolmen, 1973.

Hogan, Robert. *After the Irish Renaissance: A Critical History of the Irish Drama since "The Plough and the Stars."* Minneapolis: U. of Minnesota Press, 1967.

Holloway, Joseph. *Impressions of a Dublin Play-goer*. July–September, 1929. Vol. 1, ms. 1927. National Library of Ireland.

O'Reilly, Sr. Veronica. "Vision and Form in the Works of Denis Johnston." Diss. U. of Toronto, 1980.

Ronsley, Joseph, ed. *Denis Johnston: A Retrospective*. Gerrards Cross: Colin Smythe, 1981.

St. Peter, Christine. "Denis Johnston, the Abbey and the Spirit of the Age." *Irish University Review* 17:2 (Autumn 1987): 187–206.

MAJOR WORKS CITED IN PLAY

Blake, William. "Marriage of Heaven and Hell." In *The Complete Poetry and Prose of William Blake*. Ed. David V. Erdman. Berkeley: U. of California Press, 1982.

Dublin Book of Irish Verse 1728–1909. Ed. John Cooke. Dublin: Hodges, Figgis and Co., 1909.

Eliot, T. S. *Collected Poems 1909–1962*. London: Faber and Faber, 1963.

Gregory, Lady Augusta. *The Collected Plays of Lady Gregory*. Ed. Ann Saddlemyer. Gerrards Cross: Colin Smythe, 1970.

Joyce, James. *Ulysses*. Ed. Hans Walter Gabler. New York: Random House, 1986.

O'Casey, Sean. *Collected Plays*. 4 vols. London: Macmillan, 1949–50.

Rabelais. *Gargantua and Pantagruel*. Trans., Sir Thomas Urquhart and Peter Le Motteux. London: David Nutt, 1900.

Shaw, George Bernard. *Collected Plays*. 7 vols. London: Bodley Head, 1970–74.

Wilde, Oscar. *De Profundis*. London: Methuen, 1905.

Yeats, W. B. *Collected Plays*. London: Macmillan, 1934.

———. *Collected Poems*. London: Macmillan, 1933.

THE OLD LADY SAYS "NO!"

*A Romantic Play in Two Parts
with Choral Interludes*

OPUS ONE

One of the best loved figures of Irish romantic literature is Robert Emmet. The story of his rebellion of 1803 has all of the elements that make for magic. It was very high-minded, and completely unsuccessful. It was picturesquely costumed and insufficiently organized. Its leader—a young protestant university man of excellent social background—having failed to achieve anything more than an armed street riot, remained behind to bid goodbye to his forbidden sweetheart, instead of taking flight as any sensible rebel should do. In consequence of this, he was captured by an ogre of melodrama called Major Sirr, and was hanged after making one of the finest speeches from the dock in the annals of the criminal courts—and we have had some pretty good ones in Ireland.

So we all love Robert Emmet. Yeats and De Valera loved him, each in his own fashion. I do too; and so did Sarah Curran. Even the hoardings along the Canal have been known to display a chalked inscription, 'UP EMMET'. We all agree that it was a pity that some of his supporters had to murder one of the most liberal judges on the bench, Lord Kilwarden, and that the only practical outcome of his affray was to confirm the Union with England for about a hundred and twenty years. Our affection is not affected by these details.

The tragedy of his love has been immortalized by Tom Moore in one of his finest ballads:

> She is far from the land
> Where her young hero sleeps,
> And lovers around her are sighing.
> But coldly she turns from their gaze, and weeps,
> For her heart in his grave is lying.

Who cares that this reason for her absence from the land is the fact that she subsequently married an English officer, and ended her days happily with him elsewhere? For us, her heart will always be lying in Robert's grave. And lying is the operative word.

The whole episode has got that delightful quality of storybook unreality that creates a glow of satisfaction without any particular reference to the facts of life. To put it into conflict with those facts ought to be an easy proposition in the theatre, and particularly so back in 1926, when several years of intermittent and unromantic civil war and soured us all a little towards the woes of Cathleen ni Houlihan. It was inevitable that such a play would be written in Ireland by someone or other at about that time.

Although it is by no means my favourite play, and is my only work that might fairly be described as anti-Irish, it is by far the best spoken-of in its native habitat. In Dublin it is now generally regarded as a strongly nationalistic piece, full of sound popular sentiments and provided with a title calculated to annoy Lady Gregory and the Abbey Theatre. It is true that on the occasion of its first production at the Gate, some tentative efforts were made to have me prosecuted—for what, I cannot at present remember. But those days are long past, and the only acrimony that the play evokes today is among the cast, the older members of which argue strongly during rehearsals over business and movements that were used on previous occasions, and must not now be altered.

As for the title, I cannot be held responsible for this. It was written by somebody on a sheet of paper attached to the front of the first version, when it came back to me from the Abbey. Whether it was intended to inform me that the play had been rejected, or whether it was being offered as an alternative to my own coy little name for the play—*Shadowdance*—is a question that I never liked to ask. So it remained, thereafter, as the title of the work—a definite improvement for which I have always been grateful. Lennox Robinson used to complain bitterly about any suggestion that Lady G. was against the play, but all I know of the matter is the distaste she expressed to me in the back sitting-room of her hotel in Harcourt Street. I was never invited to Gort.

It is, of course, a director's play, written very much in the spirit of 'Let's see what would happen' if we did this or that. We were tired of the conventional three-act shape, of conversational dialogue, and of listening to the tendentious social sentiments of the stage of the 'twenties, and we wanted to know whether the emotional appeal of music could be made use of in terms of theatrical prose, and an opera constructed that did not have to be sung. Could dialogue be used in lieu of some of the scenery, or as a shorthand form of character-delineation? Could the associations and thought-patterns already connected with the songs and slogans of our city be used deliberately to evoke a planned reaction from a known audience?

The opening playlet—which was felt by Lady G. to be an all-too-brief preliminary to a vein of "coarseness" that was to follow—is made up almost entirely from lines by Mangan, Moore, Ferguson, Kickham, Todhunter, and the romantic school of nineteenth-century Irish poets, still well known to everybody although no longer imitated. So too, the final speech of the play contains some easily recognizable sections of Pearse's funeral oration for O'Donovan Rossa, together with a large portion of Emmet's actual speech from the dock, which concludes:

'When my country takes her place amongst the nations of the earth, then, and not till then, let my epitaph be written.'

There are both handicaps and benefits to be derived from writing for so specialized an audience. A phrase such as 'When in the course of human events' will spontaneously call up an association-pattern when uttered in the United States, where it belongs. An Englishman, prodded with the expression 'Kiss me, Hardy', may react in a variety of ways, but some response is usually noticeable. On the other hand, outside Ireland, a reference to 'my four beautiful green fields' will not wring any withers, but becomes instead a mere literary reference that may or may not be recognized as an echo from Yeats.

Thus, although written in a language common to all three countries, *The Old Lady* is not quite the same play in London or New York as it is in Dublin. Across the sea its intentional clichés are no longer clichés, and the various daggers concealed within its lacy sentiments find no flesh into which to probe. For this reason, apart from one production in New York, a couple in London, and a few presentations in colleges with *avant garde* theatre departments, it has never been performed outside Ireland. There the pattern devised by Hilton Edwards and Micheál MacLiammóir for its first production in 1929 has become as much an integral part of the play as is the text.

Although many of its expressionist tricks are now commonplace, especially in radio production, it was, at the time of writing, a fairly original type of play, and technically it owes less to other dramatists than anything that I have written since. The play's actual foster parents are neither Evreinov, O'Neill nor Georg Kaiser. Nor has Joyce got much to do with it, although I gratefully acknowledge the presence of his finger in the stirring of some of my later pies. I have once or twice been written to by students of the drama who feel that they can trace the influence of *Finnegans Wake* upon *The Old Lady*. This is a book that I first attempted to read through about ten years ago, and the only part of it that has got into my play did so by a most circuitous route. This is the *Thuartpeatrick* phrase, misspelled *St Peetrick* by me in the party scene. Its presence there is a surprising reminder that Tuohy, the artist who painted both Joyce and his old father, had sentences from Joyce's own lips that he was bandying around Dublin as early as the Nine Arts Ball of 1925. In this very second-hand condition the expression has found its way into my text, as a quotation from a section of a book that had then hardly been begun. There are, of course, two short quotes from *Ulysses* in *The Old Lady*, together with a phrase or two, such as 'Jacobs Vobiscuits'. But any resemblances to the *Wake* have nothing to do with me.

The two plays to which this experiment does owe something are, firstly, Kaufman and Connelly's *Beggar on Horseback*—a superb piece of American expressionism that I have always admired—and secondly, a Continental satire called *The Land of Many Names* that I once saw in the 'twenties. Who wrote it, and where it came from, I have often since wondered. I think it may have been one of the Capeks.

Southampton, Massachusetts, 1960.

THE OLD LADY
SAYS "NO!"

PERSONS

SARAH CURRAN *and* FLOWER WOMAN*
THE SPEAKER (ROBERT EMMET)
FIRST REDCOAT *and* GENERAL*
SECOND REDCOAT
MAJOR SIRR *and* GRATTAN*
STAGE HAND *and* MINISTER FOR ARTS AND CRAFTS*
DOCTOR
BLIND MAN
CHORUS: *Voices and Forms, Newsboys, Passer-By, Bus Man, Flapper, Medical, Well-Dressed Woman, Businessman, Carmel, Bernadette, An Older Man, Two Touts, Handshakers, Younger Man, A Man, Second Man, Joe, Maeve, Lady Trimmer, O'Cooney, O'Mooney, O'Rooney, Minister's Wife, He, She.*
FIRST SHADOW, SECOND SHADOW, THIRD SHADOW, FOURTH SHADOW.
*Both characters to be played by the same performer.
The action of the play opens in the garden of The Priory, the home of John Philpot Curran, close to Rathfarnham (now a suburb of Dublin), on the night of August 25th, 1803.

PART ONE

[To the left the dark gable of a building can be seen with a light burning behind the blind in the first-floor window. It is the house of John Philpot Curran,[1] The Priory, close to Rathfarnham, a village outside Dublin. To the centre and to the right are the trees of the garden, and behind them the profile of Kilmashogue[2] and the hills beyond. It is the night of August 25th in the year 1803, and the sound of men's voices is dying away into the distance as the Curtain rises.]

VOICES

With their pikes in good repair,
Says the Shan Van Vocht,
To the Curragh of Kildare
The boys they will repair,
And Lord Edward will be there,
Says the Shan Van Vocht.[3]

[The window opens and SARAH CURRAN gazes out towards the mountains.]

SARAH

The air is rich and soft—the air is mild and bland.
Her woods are tall and straight, grove rising over grove.
Trees flourish in her glens below and on her heights above,
Oh, the fair hills of Eire, oh.[4]

---

1. "Curran" Irish Parliamentarian and patriot (1750–1817) who, with Grattan, urged parliamentary reform and Catholic emancipation, and as a lawyer defended leaders of the 1798 Rising.
2. "Kilmashogue" Mountain south of Dublin visible to Sarah Curran from her Rathfarnham home.
3. "With their pikes . . . Shan Van Vocht." Famous patriotic ballad written in 1796, this version by Michael Doheny. The *Sean Bhean Bhocht* or "poor old woman" is the traditional symbol for Ireland. See note 73 below.
4. "The air is rich. . . . Eire, oh." Lines paraphrased from "The Fair Hills of Eiré, O!" by Donogh MacCon-Mara. Here and throughout this play Johnston adapted his sources freely.

Down from the high cliffs the rivulet is teeming
To wind around the willow banks that lure him from above.
Ah, where the woodbines with sleepy arms have wound him . . .[5]

[*She starts.*]

Who is there? I heard a rustling in the trees!
Who is there, I say?

[*The* SPEAKER *emerges from among the trees. He is dressed as Robert Emmet in a green tunic, white-plumed hat, white breeches and Wellington boots with gold tassels. At his side hangs a large cavalry sword.*][6]

SPEAKER [*with an appropriate gesture*] Hush beloved, it is I.

SARAH Robert! I think, oh my love, 'tis thy voice from the kingdom of souls![7]

SPEAKER Was ever light of beauty shed on loveliness like thine![8]

SARAH Oh, Robert, Robert, why have you ventured down? You are in danger.

SPEAKER My bed was the ground, my roof the greenwood above: and the wealth that I sought, one far, kind glance from my love.[9]

SARAH My love, for a vision of fanciful bliss to barter thy calm life of labour and peace![10]

SPEAKER What matters life! Deirdre is mine: she is my queen, and no man now can rob me![11]

SARAH The redcoats are everywhere. Last night they were around the house and they will come again.

SPEAKER Let them come! A million a decade![12] Let me

5. "Down from the High Cliffs . . . wound him . . . " "Serenade of a Loyal Martyr," George Darley (1795–1846).

6. "He is dressed . . . cavalry sword." This uniform still serves as regalia for the National Irish Foresters.

7. "I think, oh my love . . . of souls" "At the mid hour of night," Thomas Moore (1779–1852).

8. "Was ever light . . . like thine!" "An Ancient Tale," John O'Hagan, *nom de plume* Sliabh Cuilinn (1822–1890).

9. "My bed . . . from my love" "The Outlaw of Loch Lene," translated from the Irish by Jeremiah Joseph Callanan (1795–1829).

10. "for a vision . . . peace!" Paraphrased from "Hy Brasail—the Isle of the Blest," Gerald Griffin (1803–1840).

11. "Deirdre is mine . . . rob me!" *Deirdre* (p. 202), W. B. Yeats (1865–1939).

12. "Let them come . . . a decade!" "The Exodus," Lady Wilde, *nom de plume* Speranza (1824?–1896).

be persuaded that my springing soul may meet the eagle on the hills, and I am free.[13]

SARAH Ah, go, forget me. Why should sorrow o'er that brow a shadow fling?[14]

SPEAKER My strong ones have fallen from the bright eye of day.[15] Their graves are red, but their souls are with God in glory.[16]

SARAH Ah, love, love! Where is thy throne? It is gone in the wind![17]

SPEAKER A dark chain of silence is thrown o'er the deep.[18] No streak of dawning is in the sky. It is still unriven, that clanking chain.[19] Yet, am I the slave they say?[20]

SARAH A lost dream to us now in our home! Ullagone! Gall to our heart![21]

SPEAKER But there is lightning in my blood—red lightning tightening in my blood! Oh, if there was a sword in every Irish hand! If there was a flame in every Irish heart to put an end to slavery and shame! Oh, I would end these things![22]

SARAH It is too late! Large, large affliction unto me and mine, that one of his majestic bearing, his fair and stately form, should thus be tortured and o'erborne—that this unsparing storm should wreak its wrath on head like this![23]

SPEAKER [softly] My earthly comforter, whose love so indefeasible might be![24] Your holy, delicate, white hands shall girdle me with steel. You'll pray for me, my flower of flowers! You'll think of me through daylight hours, my virgin flower![25]

SARAH At least I'll love thee till I die.

---

13. "Let me be persuaded . . . free." "Sonnet Written during His Residence in College," Charles Wolfe (1791–1823).

14. "Ah, go . . . a shadow fling?" "Go! Forget Me," Wolfe.

15. "My strong ones . . . eye of day." "Oh, Say, My Brown Drimin," Callanan.

16. "Their graves . . . glory!" "Plorans Ploravit," Sir Aubrey De Vere (1814–1902).

17. "Where is thy throne . . . the wind!" "Gone in the Wind," Mangan.

18. "A dark chain . . . o'er the deep." "Eiré," William Drennan (1754–1820).

19. "No streak . . . clanking chain." "To Erin," Mary Eva Kelly (1825?–?).

20. "Yet, am I the slave they say?" "Soggarth Aroon," John Banim (1798–1842).

21. "A lost dream . . . Gall to our Heart!" "The Swan's Lament for the Desolation of Lir," John Todhunter (1839–1916).

22. "But there is lightning . . . end these things!" "Dark Rosaleen," Mangan.

23. "It is too late! . . . its wrath on head like this!" "O'Hussey's Ode to Maguire," Mangan.

24. "My earthly comforter . . . might be!" "True Loveliness," Darley.

25. "Your holy . . . virgin flower!" "Dark Rosaleen."

SPEAKER How long, ah, Sarah, can I say how long my life will last?

SARAH Cease boding doubt, my gentlest love; be hushed that struggling sigh.[26]

SPEAKER When he who adores thee has left but a name, ah say, wilt thou weep?[27]

SARAH I shall not weep. I shall not breathe his name.[28] For my heart in his grave will be lying.[29] I shall sing a lament for the Sons of Usnach.[30]

SPEAKER But see, she smiles, she smiles! Her rosy mouth dimples with hope and joy; her dewy eyes are full of pity![31]

SARAH Ah, Robert, Robert, come to me.

SPEAKER [*climbing up*] I have written my name in letters of fire across the page of history. I have unfurled the green flag in the streets and cried aloud from the high places to all the people of the Five Kingdoms.[32] 'Men of Eire, awake to be blest! Rise, Arch of the Ocean and Queen of the West!'[33] I have dared all for Ireland and I will dare all again for Sarah Curran. Ah, it is a glorious thing to dare![34]

[*He is about to touch her outstretched hand when*—]

A VOICE Halt! Who goes there?

SARAH Ah God! The yeomen!

VOICES The countersign.

     Stand.

     Front point.

     Advance.[35]

SPEAKER The flint-hearted Saxon![36]

---

26. "At least I'll love . . . struggling sigh!" "Dry be that Tear," Richard Brinsley Sheridan (1751–1816).

27. "When he . . . thou weep?" "When he who adores thee," Moore.

28. "I shall no weep . . . his name." "Oh! breathe not his name," Moore.

29. "For my heart . . . will be lying." "She is far from the land," Moore.

30. "I shall sing . . . Usnach!" "Deirdre's Great Lamentation for the Sons of Usnach," Todhunter.

31. "But see . . . full of pity!" "The Benumbed Butterfly," A. De Vere.

32. "I have written . . . the Five Kingdoms" This passage appears to be Johnston's own composition, but in margin on leaf 32 of *Beta* Yeats remarked: "This is nonsense, but if by Tom Moore it should remain."

33. "Men of Eiré . . . Queen of the West!" "Eiré," Drennan.

34. "I have dared all . . . thing to dare!" Adapted from G. B. Shaw's *Saint Joan*, 6:115, 154.

35. "The countersign . . . Advance." "Rory of the Hill," Charles Joseph Kickham (1828–1882).

36. "The flint-hearted Saxon" See note 15.

[*He makes a gesture to her. She disappears and the light goes out.*]

SARAH . . . in their fearful red array!³⁷

FIRST REDCOAT [*rushing forward*] Hold! Surrender or I fire!

SECOND REDCOAT We hold this house for our lord the King.

FIRST REDCOAT Amen, says I. May all traitors swing.³⁸

SPEAKER [*springing down and folding his arms*] Slaves and dastards, stand aside!³⁹

[MAJOR SIRR *enters.*]

SIRR Spawn of treason,⁴⁰ bow down thy humbled head to him, the King!⁴¹

SPEAKER A nation's voice, a nation's voice, 'tis stronger than the King.⁴²

SIRR Silence rebel! Do you not know who I am?

SPEAKER A jackal of the Pale.⁴³

SIRR Major Sirr.

SPEAKER Who trapped Lord Edward?⁴⁴

SIRR The same.

SPEAKER [*drawing his sword*] I am honoured. Ireland will remember. Look well to your soul, Major Sirr, for the dawn of the Gael is still to break; when they that are up will be down and they that are down will be up.⁴⁵ I tell you, Major Sirr, we'll be a glorious nation yet—redeemed, erect, alone!

[*He leaps upon them. One of the* REDCOATS *clubs his musket and strikes him a resounding blow upon the head. The lights flicker*

37. " . . . fearful red array" "Kathleen bán Adair," Francis Davis (1810–1885).

38. "We hold this house . . . all traitors swing." "The Croppy Boy, A Ballad of '98," William B. McBurney, *nom de plume* Carroll Malone.

39. "Slaves and . . . aside!" "Fag an Bealach," Charles Gavan Duffy (1816–1903).

40. "Spawn of treason" "Oliver's Advice," Colonel William Blacker (1777–1855).

41. "bow down . . . the King!" "The Land Betrayed," Sir Stephen E. De Vere (1812–1904).

42. "A Nation's . . . the King." "Nationality," Thomas Osborne Davis (1814–1845).

43. "A jackal of the Pale" Sycophant of the British. The Pale, here synonymous with Dublin, was the only part of Ireland under English domination before the time of Oliver Cromwell.

44. "Lord Edward" Fitzgerald, a slain leader of the 1798 Rising.

45. "when they . . . down will be up." *The Rising of the Moon* (p. 67), Lady Augusta Gregory (1852–1932).

momentarily and he lies still. SARAH CURRAN *appears once more at the window.*]

SARAH A star is gone! There is a blank in heaven.[46] The last great tribune of the world is dead.[47]

SIRR [*seemingly a little surprised*]

The sport of fools—the scoff of knaves,

Dead ere they blossomed, barren, blighted.

They came, whose counsels wrapped the land in foul rebellion's flame,

Their hearts unchastened by remorse, their cheeks untinged by shame,[48]

To sue for a pity they shall not—shall not—[49]

Er—

[*One of the* REDCOATS *kneels beside the* SPEAKER *and shakes him by the shoulder.* SIRR *looks helplessly into the wings from which he receives a whispered prompt.*]

PROMPT Find.

FIRST REDCOAT Ay!

SECOND REDCOAT What's up?

SIRR [*to the wings*] Curtain . . . curtain . . . I say.

STAGE HAND Is he hurted?

VOICES He's hurt. Hurt. He's hurt. Hurted.

FIRST REDCOAT It wasn't my fault. I only . . .

SIRR Curtain, please. Do stand back for a moment and give him a chance.

VOICES Loosen his collar. What do you think you're doing? How did it happen? What's the matter? He'll be all right. Give him brandy. Take those boots off. Stand back, please. Did you see the skelp he gave him? Can I help?

[*The Curtain comes jerkily down and there is a heavy tramping behind upon the stage. Presently* SIRR *comes through the Curtain. House lights up.*]

SIRR [*beckoning to someone in the audience*] Is there a doctor in . . . I say . . . can you?

DOCTOR Me?

46. "A star is gone! . . . in heaven." "The Fallen Star," Darley.
47. "The last . . . is dead." "The Great Tribune," Denis Florence McCarthy (1817–1882).
48. "The sport of fools . . . untinged by shame" See note 41.
49. "To sue for a pity they shall not" "The Ballad of the Bier that Conquered; or O'Donnell's Answer," A. De Vere.

SIRR Just come through for a minute. I think he'll be all right.

DOCTOR It looked a heavy enough . . .

SIRR I don't think it is . . .

DOCTOR . . . blow from the front.

SIRR . . . very serious, really.

DOCTOR I hope not. Anyhow you had better see whether you can't . . .

[*They disappear through the Curtain, talking. Presently* SIRR *re-appears.*]

SIRR Ladies and gentlemen . . . he . . . er . . . the doctor would like the curtain up again . . . the draught blows through from the scene dock when it's across. We're really very sorry that the performance should be held up . . . but you see . . . it's nothing really . . . He . . . er . . . says he will be all right in a moment if he's kept quiet and not moved . . . if you would only be so good as to keep your seats and stay perfectly quiet for a few moments . . . just a few moments . . . while the doctor is . . . er . . . busy . . . I'm sure we'll be able to go on . . . if you don't mind . . . curtain please . . . quite quiet please . . . just for a few minutes . . . thank you so much.

[*He hurries off. The Curtain is slowly drawn again, disclosing the* SPEAKER *where we left him, now attended by the* DOCTOR, *the* STAGE HAND *and one of the* REDCOATS. *A black gauze curtain has been drawn behind him through which we can see dim figures moving about and hear the thumping of heavy weights.*]

DOCTOR That's better now. Can you get them off?

STAGE HAND Yes, sir. They're coming now.

[*He draws off one of the* SPEAKER'S *boots.*]

REDCOAT How could I know anyway? It wasn't my fault. I tell you I only . . .

DOCTOR That's all right. Hold up his head a little. That's better. Oh, they've got it up.

[*He refers to the Curtain.*]

REDCOAT Ah, God, isn't it awful!

DOCTOR Ask those people to keep quiet there while he's coming round.

STAGE HAND Ay, Barnie, tell them to shut up! Give us a hand with this boot. I can't get a grip on it at all.

REDCOAT I don't know how it could have happened at all. You pull now.

STAGE HAND Ah, will you hold on? How the hell . . .

DOCTOR Ssssssh!

STAGE HAND There she comes.

DOCTOR See if you can get something to cover his legs with. He must be kept warm. And ask them to turn down that light a bit. He'll be all right soon if he's kept quiet and allowed to come round.

[*The* STAGE HAND *goes out obligingly.*]

REDCOAT I swear to God I hit him no harder than I was shown yesterday. I only . . . look . . .

DOCTOR Ah, be quiet you, and be off. You're more of a hindrance than a help.

REDCOAT It's all very well blaming me, but I only did what I was shown bef . . .

DOCTOR Ssssssh!

[*The* REDCOAT *goes off muttering protestations. The lights are dimmed, making the forms behind the gauze clearer still. Presently the* STAGE HAND *enters with a pair of gaudy carpet slippers.*]

STAGE HAND Would these be any use? They were all I could find. They belong to Mr . . . er . . .

DOCTOR He's stirring a little.

[*He examines the* SPEAKER *while the* STAGE HAND *puts the slippers on his feet.*]

STAGE HAND Is the lights O.K. now?

DOCTOR What's that? Oh, fine. You'd better . . .

STAGE HAND I brought a sup of brandy.

DOCTOR Brandy! Good heavens, no! He has a slight concussion.

STAGE HAND Is that a fact? A what?

DOCTOR But I tell you what. Go and see if you can manage to get a little ice.

STAGE HAND [*dubiously*] An ice?

DOCTOR Yes. You know. In a basin of cold water. For a compress.

STAGE HAND Oh, for a . . . Oh I see.

[*He goes out slowly.*]

DOCTOR And . . . [*He notices the slippers.*] My God, what are those? I told you to bring something for his legs. Do you hear? A rug. [*He rises and crosses.*] Has anybody got a rug? [*He goes off and his voice is heard faintly.*] A rug for his legs. Ah, thanks so much. That will . . .

[*Silence. The figures behind the Curtain have ceased to move and are clustered in a silent group peering through towards the spot where the* SPEAKER *is lying. Presently the latter stirs and his lips begin to move. There is a dim and distant boom-boom-boom as of someone tapping on a big drum. The lights pulse.*]

SPEAKER Redeemious . . . Oh . . . be a redeemious . . . re . . . warmest core I said . . . we'll [*He opens his eyes and stares weakly ahead.*] . . . I love thee . . . love thee bosom my head bosom my head's all . . . Oh, God! [*There is a pause while he stares out into the auditorium.*] They that are down will be down . . . down . . . up . . . erect . . . redeemiable . . . love thee, Sarah . . . redeemiablecurran . . . I see you. [*Pause—then with a great effort.*] I am the Speaker . . . Deadbosom I see you.

THE FORMS [*answering on behalf of the audience with unctuous friendliness*]

A. Quirke present	H. Dwyer present
B. Quinn present	I. Burke present
C. Foley present	J. Farrell present
D. Byrne present	K. Gleeson present
E. Ryan present	L. Mooney present
F. Carrol present	M. Quigley present
G. Lynch present	

SPEAKER [*holding up his hand peremptorily*] Stop! [*Pause. He bows solemnly.*] Thank you.

THE FORMS [*whispering in rhythm*]
Poor poor poor poor
Hit him hit him
With a gun
Butt end butt end
Dirty dirty
Give him water
For a compress
Calf's foot jelly
Fever fever
Ninety-nine point ninety ninety
Fahrenheit Centigrade
Centigrade Fahrenheit
Very unsettled unsettled unsettled
Take his boots off
Milk and soda

> Patrick Dun's[50] and
> Cork Street[51] Mater[52]
> Adelaide[53] and
> Vincent's[54] Elpis[55]
> Baggot Street[56] and
> Mercer's[57] Meath[58] and
> Is he better?
> How's the headache?
> Ambulance ambulance
> S.O.S.
> S.O.S. S.O.S.
> Tut tut tut tut
> Tut tut tut tut
> Poor poor poor poor . . .

SPEAKER [*with an impatient flap of his hand*] Slaves and dastards stand aside, a nation's voice . . . nation's voice is stronger than a Speaker . . . I am an honoured gloriable nationvoice your Sirrflinthearted Saxons . . . Oh! . . . if it would only stop going round . . . round . . . round . . . up . . . down . . . up will be down . . . O God, I am the Unspeakerable.

THE FORMS [*relentlessly*]
> On with the performance
> Programmes Tenpence
> No Smoking
> Spitting Coughing
> Nobody admitted
> Till after the Performance
> After nine
> Point ninety ninety
> For further particulars
> Apply to the Manager
> N. Moore

---

50. "Patrick Dun's" Sir Patrick Dun's Hospital, Grand Canal Street. In notes 50–58, all addresses from 1920s, time of play's composition.
51. "Cork Street" Cork Street Dental Hospital.
52. "Mater" Mater Misericordiae, a charity hospital on Eccles Street.
53. "Adelaide" Adelaide Hospital and Charity Clinics, Peter Street.
54. "Vincent's" St. Vincent's Hospital and Dispensary, Stephen's Green.
55. "Elpis" Dublin Nursing home on Lower Mount Street.
56. "Baggot Street" The Royal City of Dublin Hospital, Upper Baggot Street.
57. "Mercer's" Mercer's Hospital, William Street.
58. "Meath" Meath Hospital, Heytesbury Street.

O. Callan

Q. O'Reilly

R. Donovan

S. Muldoon

SPEAKER [*with the rhythm*] Yes . . . yes . . . yes . . . yes . . .

THE FORMS T. Cosgrave

U. O'Toole

V. Kelly

W. Fogarty

SPEAKER

Red lightning tightening through my blood

Red tightening lightning tightening through my blood

My tightening blood . . .

[*The voices are merged in a clanking, shrieking concatenation that swells up . . . the throb of petrol engines, the hoot of motor horns, the rattle and pounding of lorries, and, above all, the cry of the newsboys.*]

NEWSBOYS Hegler Press

Late Buff Hegler Press[59]

Weekly Honesty[60]

Hegler Press

SPEAKER [*commencing to act again, at the top of his voice*] Their graves are red but their souls are with God in glory. A dark chain of silence is thrown o'er the deep. Silence . . . silence I say. O Ireland, Ireland, it is still unriven, that clanking chain . . . still unriven. O Ireland, Ireland, no streak of dawning is in the sky.

[*As he has been declaiming the crowd breaks up and passes to and fro as in the street. The gauze parts. Headlights of motor cars. A policeman with a white baton is directing the traffic, while behind him upon a pedestal stands GRATTAN[61] with arm outstretched. He has the face of MAJOR SIRR.*]

SPEAKER [*now in the midst of the traffic*] Men of Eire, awake to be blest! Do you hear? [*He fiercely accosts a PASSER-BY.*] Do you hear? Awake!

PASSER-BY [*politely disengaging himself*] Sorry. The banks close at half two.

59. "Late Buff Hegler" Buff-colored edition of the *Dublin Evening Herald.*

60. "Weekly Honesty" Dublin Journal of the 1920's.

61. "upon a pedestal stands Grattan" This statue still faces Trinity College from College Green, one of central Dublin's major thoroughfares.

SPEAKER At the loud call of freedom why don't they awake? Come back! . . . Rise Arch of the Ocean . . . Let me be persuaded that my springing soul may meet the eagle on the hills . . . the hills . . . the hills . . . I say . . . [*He shouts.*] I say! Look here!

[*The* STAGE HAND *enters with the script.*]

STAGE HAND What's the trouble?

SPEAKER The hills!

STAGE HAND What hills?

SPEAKER Yes, what hills? Where?

STAGE HAND Where's which?

SPEAKER Don't be so stupid. You know I must have them. The eagle on the . . .

STAGE HAND Did the Artistic Director say you were to have hills?

SPEAKER I don't know what you mean. I can't go on like this. This is not right.

STAGE HAND Well it's the first I heard of it. Wait now till I get the place.

SPEAKER Down from the high cliff the rivulet is teeming. Go away! Be off!

STAGE HAND Where had you got to?

SPEAKER Not very far. I was with Sarah. She was up there. I was talking to her.

STAGE HAND [*producing a dirty programme*] Scene One. Wait now till I see. Who did you say you were?

SPEAKER Robert Emmet. See there.

STAGE HAND Oh is that you? I though I rekernized the unyform.

SPEAKER 'The action of the play opens in the garden of "The Priory", the home of John Philpot Curran close to Rathfarnham.' You see. This is not Rathfarnham.

STAGE HAND No. I suppose not.

SPEAKER I can't go on here. Can't you stop this noise?

STAGE HAND Well you know I'd be glad to do all I can, but . . . well, you see, it's all very well telling me now.

SPEAKER The air is rich and soft, the air is mild and bland, her woods are tall and straight, grove rising over grove . . .

STAGE HAND Yes, I know, but I don't know what I can do. You should have told me sooner. You see the shops is all shut now . . .

SPEAKER And Sarah . . . Sarah Curran is gone too. Clear all this away!

STAGE HAND Ay, you can't touch that! That's wanted for the dancing class.[62]

SPEAKER Stop them! My play! Rathfarnham!

STAGE HAND Ah you know I'm doing my best for you. But as a matter of fact I have to be off now.

SPEAKER Off where?

STAGE HAND I'm due at my Irish class[63] this half hour.

SPEAKER And what am I to do?

STAGE HAND Ah sure aren't you doing well enough. You're very particular all of a sudden.

SPEAKER Come back, damn you!

STAGE HAND Ah, they won't know the difference. It's good enough for that gang.[64] Ta-ta now or I'll be late.

SPEAKER Stop! You must tell me . . .

STAGE HAND You'll get a Rathfarnham bus over there at the corner. Goodbye-ee!

[*He goes.*]

SPEAKER Here! Oh my head! At the corner where? Rathfarnham.

BUS MAN Rathfarnham bus.[65] No. 17 Rathfarnham. Step along now please.

SPEAKER Are you going to Rathfarnham?

BUS MAN This bus's full. Full, I tell ya. You'll have to wait for the next.

SPEAKER Nonsense . . . there's lots of room. See . . .

BUS MAN The bus's full. D'ye want to get me into trouble? Let go the bar now there's room for no more here. There'll be another along behind.

62. "That's wanted for the dancing class." The Abbey had acting, singing, and dancing schools that used the annex in which the play was being presented in 1929.

63. "Irish class" The Gaelic League, founded in 1893 by Douglas Hyde and Eoin MacNeill, was, by the time of Johnston's youth, a well-organized, nation-wide pressure group that had as its aim the restoration of Irish as the spoken language of Ireland. Besides its language classes, it taught history, dancing, drama, and generally promoted national self-reliance.

64. "that gang" The play's audience in 1929, in the 102-seat Peacock Theatre, consisting mainly of young Dubliners interested in avant-garde theatre or their elders determined to promote cultural events. Joseph Holloway, inveterate Dublin theatre-goer, described Johnston's play and its audience on thirty-nine pages of his journal, evidence of the play's impact.

65. "Rathfarnham bus" The tram of the early versions became anachronistic after 1949 when Dublin replaced its last tram.

SPEAKER I tell you there's nobody there.

[*Ding Ding Ding.*]

BUS MAN Fares please. [*And he moves off mysteriously.*]

SPEAKER There's nobody there! Liar! Cheat! You're all a lot of . . . a lot of . . . I shall speak to the stage manager about . . . [*His voice breaks.*] Oh my head! I wish I wasn't so tired. I wish I wasn't so terribly tired!

[*He sinks down upon something in the centre of the stage. The passers-by thin out and the noise dies away, first into a low hum and then into complete silence. There is nobody left but the figure of GRATTAN and an old tattered FLOWER WOMAN in a black straw hat who sits crouching at the base of the pedestal.*]

SPEAKER [*mumbling*] My bed was the ground—my way the greenwood above, and the wealth I sought . . . I sought . . . the wealth . . . Oh, what is it?

GRATTAN How long, O Lord, how long?[66]

[*Pause.*]

SPEAKER [*without looking round*] What was that?

GRATTAN This place stifles me. The thick, sententious atmosphere of this little hell of babbling torment![67] Sometimes the very breath seems to congeal in my throat and I can scarce keep from choking.

SPEAKER [*nodding gravely*] I might have known it.

WOMAN Penny a bunch th' violets.

GRATTAN God forgive me, but it is hard sometimes. Very hard.

SPEAKER All the same I will not allow this. It is the voice of Major Sirr. It is not my part.

GRATTAN Your part? Ah yes! More play-acting. Go on, go on.

SPEAKER I am Robert Emmet and I . . .

GRATTAN A young man playing Robert Emmet! Yes, yes, they all come here.[68]

SPEAKER I am Robert Emmet. I have written my name

66. "How long, O Lord, how long?" Curtain line of G. B. Shaw's *Saint Joan*, 6:208, and borrowed by Shaw from T. B. Macaulay's "The Marriage of Tirzah and Ahirad."

67. "this little hell of babbling torment" Conflation of several statements of Father Keegan in G. B. Shaw's *John Bull's Other Island*, 2:923, 983, 1015.

68. "Yes, yes, they all come here." Grattan is referring to Trinity College, where Emmet himself was an undergraduate at the time of his insurrection in 1803.

in letters of fire across the page of history. I have unfurled the green flag . . .

GRATTAN Letters of fire?

SPEAKER Their graves are red but their souls . . .

GRATTAN Ah yes, the graves are red . . . the grave of one poor helpless old man, the justest judge in Ireland . . . dragged from his coach by the mob and slaughtered in the road.

SPEAKER Kilwarden![69]

GRATTAN Kilwarden's grave is red.

SPEAKER Who said that? I did my best to save him, but the people were mad . . .

GRATTAN 'Let no man perish in consequence of my death,' he cried, as his lifeblood stained the cobbles crimson . . .

SPEAKER . . . maddened by long centuries of oppression and injustice. I did my best to save him. What more could I do?

GRATTAN 'Let no man perish, save by the regular operation of the laws.' And with that, pierced by a dozen patriot pikes, he died, at the feet of his gallant countrymen.

SPEAKER It was horrible. But it was war.

GRATTAN Eighty tattered turncocks[70] from the Coombe;[71] a plumed hat, and a silver sword. War, for the liberation of Erin!

WOMAN Me four bewtyful gre-in fields. Me four bewtyful gre-in fields.[72]

SPEAKER Men of Eire, awake to be blest!

GRATTAN The full long years of my life I gave for her, with the harness weighing on my shoulders and my heart bleeding for my country's woes.

SPEAKER Rise, Arch of the Ocean!

GRATTAN Full fifty years I worked and waited, only to see my country's new-found glory melt away at the bidding of the omniscient young Messiahs with neither the ability to work nor the courage to wait.

SPEAKER I have the courage to go on.

GRATTAN Oh, it is an easy thing to draw a sword and

---

69. "Kilwarden" Chief Justice of Ireland, the only casualty of Emmet's insurrection

70. "turncocks" Bartenders.

71. "the Coombe" Commercial area in central Dublin south of the Liffey.

72. "Me four bewtyful gre-in fields" Corruption of the lament of Yeats's eponymous heroine in *Cathleen ni Houlihan* (p. 81) whose "fields" are the four ancient provinces of Ireland: Leinster, Munster, Connacht, and Ulster.

raise a barricade. It saves working, it saves waiting. It saves everything but blood![73] And blood is the cheapest thing the good God has made.

WOMAN Two apples a penny. Penny a bunch th' gre-in fields.

SPEAKER Listen! Something is telling me that I must go on. I must march proudly through to the final act. Look! [Pointing.] The people are waiting for me, watching me.

GRATTAN Fool, fool, strutting upon the stage![74] Go out, into the cold night air, before you crucify yourself in the blind folly of your eternal play-acting.

SPEAKER [to the audience] He is an old man. He does not understand the way we do. He can only doubt . . . while we believe . . . believe with heart and soul and every fibre of our tired bodies. Therefore I am not afraid to go on. I will kiss my wounds in the last act. I will march proudly through, head high, even if it must be to my grave. That is the only test.

GRATTAN Ah, the love of death, creeping like a mist at the heels of my countrymen! Death is the only art in which we own no masters. Death is the only voice that can be heard in this distressful land where no man's word is taken, no man's message heeded, no man's prayer answered except it be his epitaph. Out into every quarter of the globe we go, seeking for a service in which to die: saving the world by dying for a good cause just as readily as we will damn it utterly by dying for a bad one. It is all the same to us. It is the only thing that we can understand.

[The WOMAN laughs shortly and shrilly and breaks into a wheezy cough.]

SPEAKER What is that woman doing here?

WOMAN God bless ye, lovely gentleman, spare a copper for a cuppa tea. Spare a copper for yer owin old lady, for when th' trouble is on me I must be talkin' te me friends.[75]

GRATTAN A copper, lovely gentleman, for your own old lady.

73. "It saves working . . . but blood!" G. B. Shaw's Larry Doyle says in *John Bull's Other Island:* "[The Irishman] dreams of what the Shan Van Vocht said in ninety-eight. If you want to interest him in Ireland youve [*sic*] got to call the unfortunate island Kathleen ni Hoolihan and pretend she's a little old woman. It saves thinking. It saves working. It saves everything except imagination . . . " (p. 910).

74. "Fool, fool, strutting upon the Stage!" Adaptation of *Macbeth* 5.5.17–28.

75. "for when th' trouble is on me I must be talkin' to me friends." *Cathleen ni Houlihan* (p. 81), Yeats.

SPEAKER Go away! There is something horrible about your voice.

GRATTAN
> Young she is, and fair she is
> And would be crowned a Queen.[76]

SPEAKER What can I do in this place? I can't even remember my lines!

WOMAN Yer lines, ducky. Ay Jack, pull them up on ye!

SPEAKER I must go back to Rathfarnham. They will understand there.

GRATTAN A shadowy land has appeared.

SPEAKER Sally!

GRATTAN
Men thought it a region of Sunshine and Rest,
And they called it 'Rathfarnham', the Land of the Blest.[77]

SPEAKER Oh if the will had wings, how fast I'd fly to the home of my heart!

GRATTAN Poor weary footsore fool. And we are all the same, every one of us, whether we look to the foreigner for our sovereign or for our salvation.[78] All of us fit to lead, and none of us fit to serve.

SPEAKER
> If wishes were power, if words were spells,
> I'd be this hour where my true love dwells![79]

GRATTAN Driven blindly on by the fury of our spurious[80] moral courage! Is there to be no rest for Ireland from her soul? What monstrous blasphemy has she committed to be condemned to drift for ever like the wandering Jew after a Heaven that can never be?

WOMAN [*crooning softly to herself*]
She's a darlin', she's a daisy
She has all the neighbours crazy,
And she's arrums an' legs upon her like a man.

---

76. "Young she is . . . crowned a Queen." "Kathleen Ny-Houlahan," Mangan.

77. "A shadowy land . . . the Land of the Blest." See note 10.

78. "foreigner for our sovereign or for our salvation" Echo of Stephen Dedalus's complaint that, as Irishman, he serves two masters: an English king and a Roman Catholic Pope (*Ulysses* 1, line 638).

79. "If wishes were power . . . my true love dwells." Children's street rhyme.

80. "spurious" Previous to the 1977 Smythe edition this read "pitiless"; this late change reveals the elderly Johnston's abandonment of his earlier belief in the power of visionary politics. See pp. 20–27 of Introduction.

But no matter where she goes,
Sure everybody knows
That she's Mick Magilligan's daughter, Mary Ann.[81]
GRATTAN In my day Dublin was the second city of a
mighty Empire. What is she now?
SPEAKER No! No!
GRATTAN [*with unutterable scorn*] Free!
[*He bursts into a wild peal of laughter.*]
SPEAKER You are lying! It is the voice of Major Sirr!
You are trying to torment me . . . torture me . . . Ghosts out
of Hell, that's what you are.
[*The figures are blotted out by black curtains which sweep across
behind the* SPEAKER, *entrapping him in their folds.*]
SPEAKER But I'm not afraid! Heads up! One allegiance
only! Robert Emmet is not afraid! I know what I want and I'm
going on. [*Feverishly fumbling with the folds.*]
God save Ireland cried the heroes,
God save Ireland cry we all,
Whether on the scaffold high—
Whether on the scaffold high
The scaffold high . . . ![82]
Come out! Come out! Where are you? Oh, where am I? Come
out! I . . . can't . . . remember . . . my lines . . . !
[*An old blind man, tap-tapping with his stick, passes slowly
across the stage, a mug outstretched and a fiddle under his arm.*]
SPEAKER If only I could get through. Where's the way
through?
[*A* FLAPPER *and a* TRINITY MEDICAL[83] *appear.*]
FLAPPER No, I don't like the floor there, the Metropole's[84]
much better. As for that Buttery[85] basement up and down and
down and up Grafton Street.[86] Tea for two[87] and two for tea on

81. "She's a darlin' . . . Mike Magilligan's daughter, Mary Ann." Johnston's favorite barroom song supplied Mary Ann Magilligan, another avatar for Cathleen ni
Houlihan. Buck Mulligan also sings this song in *Ulysses* 1, lines 382–84.
82. "God save Ireland . . . scaffold high" Anthem of Irish nationalists.
83. "Trinity Medical" Medical student at Trinity College, he and the flapper
are emblematic of Anglo-Irish (Protestant) class privilege and social frivolity.
84. "Metropole" Fashionable dance spot in the 1960s; Fuller's in the 1920–30
editions.
85. "Buttery" Student refectory at Trinity College.
86. "Grafton Street" Dublin's most expensive shopping street, running from
Trinity College to Saint Stephen's Green.
87. "Tea for two" American hit song of 1925, by Vincent Youmans and Irving
Caesar.

one enchanted evening[88] in the Dewdrop Inn.[89] Do you like my nails this shade? Heart's Despair it's called.

MEDICAL Play wing three[90] for Monkstown.[91] Four caps[92] in the last couple of seasons. Pity they've put those glass doors in the Capitol boxes.[93]

FLAPPER Brown Thomas[94] for panty-bras and Elizabeth Arden to rebuild drooping tissues. Max Factor, Chanel Number Five and Mum's the Word. Has your car got a strap round the bonnet?[95]

MEDICAL Well let's go up to Mother Mason's[96] and hold hands. She needs decarbonizing probably. Botany Bay,[97] you can be sure. Number twenty-one is my number.

SPEAKER Can I get through here?

FLAPPER Brittas Bay[98] in a yellow M.G.

SPEAKER I beg your pardon.

MEDICAL Would you like a part in the Trinity Players?[99]

SPEAKER What?

FLAPPER Tennis at Fitzwilliam[100] all through the summer. We all go to Alexandra[101] where the Lady Ardilaun lectures on Gilbert and Sullivan are quite indescribable. See you at the Carrickmines[102] Mixed Singles. The Aga Khan is playing.

88. "one enchanted evening" Song from 1949 musical *South Pacific* by Richard Rodgers and Oscar Hammerstein. Introduced in 1960 edition, this replaced "My baby's gotta red-hot body."

89. "Dewdrop Inn" A chain of bed and breakfast establishments.

90. "wing three" Rugby position.

91. "Monkstown" Wealthy suburb south of Dublin next to Dún Laoghaire.

92. "four caps" Rugby winners are awarded losing team's caps as trophies.

93. "glass doors in the Capital boxes" Closed theatre boxes were a choice private place for dating sex.

94. "Brown Thomas" Expensive department store on Grafton Street. 1932 edition read "Robert's for camibockers and the Boncilla method rebuilds drooping tissue. Houbigant, Dorin and Inecto. But I always go to Switzer's on Saturday mornings. Two banana splits, please."

95. "bonnet" Automobile hood in North American usage.

96. "Mother Mason's" Unidentifiable dating spot, appearing in all editions.

97. "Botany Bay" A Trinity college quadrangle built 1790–1816, and in Johnston's time known as the rowdiest dormitory. Students named it after the Australian convict settlement for Irish political prisoners.

98. "Brittas Bay" Picnic spot south of Dublin.

99. "Trinity Players" Amateur acting group to which Johnston belonged in the 1920s, then named Trinity Dramatic.

100. "Fitzwilliam" Exclusive lawn tennis club on Wilton Place in 1960s; 1932 edition, "tennis at Greystones."

101. "Alexandra" College and school on Earlsfort Terrace for wealthy Protestant girls, and the school of Johnston's first wife, Shelagh Richards.

102. "Carrickmines" Exclusive tennis club in the town of the same name.

MEDICAL Tyson's[103] ties tie tightly. Going to crew next week for Dr Snufflebottom. Coming in left, Wanderers. Use your feet!

BOTH [*singing as they disappear*]
Kitty she was witty, Kitty she was pretty,
Down in the valley where they tried to pull her leg.
One of the committee thought he would be witty,
So he hit her on the titty with a hard boiled egg.

SPEAKER What was that?

[*A* WELL-DRESSED WOMAN *and a* BUSINESSMAN *appear.*]

WELL-DRESSED WOMAN This is the way to the Ringsend[104] Baby Club. Double three Clubs. You are requested to attend a meeting of the Peamount[105] After-care Committee. Ballsbridge,[106] at 11:30 a.m. [*She yawns loudly.*]

BUSINESSMAN Dame Street[107] to Clarinda Park East Kingstown not Dún Laoghaire.[108] Second National Loan Deferred Preference is now at thirty under proof. And only last Saturday I went round the Island[109] in twenty-five and a bisque. Service not self I always say. Telegrams: 'Stability' Dublin. Have you got a *Herald*?

SPEAKER Please . . . please! Can't you tell me the way out of here?

WELL-DRESSED WOMAN Cover the milk. Do keep the milk covered,[110] there's a good man.

[*Goes.*]

BUSINESSMAN [*making a secret sign*] Past Grand High Deacon for the Fitzwilliam Lodge.[111] Honorary Treasurer of

103. "Tyson's" Shirtmakers on Grafton Street.
104. "Ringsend" In the 1920s, a poor section of Dublin and object of wealthy women's volunteer charity.
105. "Peamount" Tuberculosis sanitorium in Newcastle.
106. "Ballsbridge" A south central, wealthy district of Dublin where Johnston's family lived.
107. "Dame Street" Dublin's financial district.
108. "Clarinda Park East Kingstown not Dun Laoghaire." Residential street in a wealthy town south of Dublin originally called Kingstown but renamed Dún Laoghaire in 1926.
109. "Island" Dalkey Island, off coast south of Dublin.
110. "Do keep the milk covered" Milk was delivered in uncovered containers in 1920s, a health hazard women crusaded against.
111. "Fitzwilliam Lodge" Masonic lodge, fraternity for Irish Protestant businessmen.

the Sandycove and District Philatelic Society. House Committee, Royal St George. Assistant District Commissioner, South County Dublin Boy Scouts. Achievement. [*Goes.*]

[TWO YOUNG THINGS *from somewhere up Phibsboro'*[112] *way appear.*]

CARMEL Down at the Girls' Club[113] a Parnell Square. Janey Mac, such gas as we had!

BERNADETTE Ah God, if I'd only a known! I couldn't get out a Tuesday. Were the fellas in?

CARMEL They were. The Grocers' and Vintners' Assistants Association.[114] D'ye know?

BERNADETTE An' I suppose you had the Wet Dreams[115] to play?

CARMEL We had. The Gorgeous Wrecks were on in the Banba Hall. But listen. D'ye know the fella out a Cusack's a Dorset Street?

BERNADETTE Is it that awful-lookin' iabeck[116] with the red hair?

CARMEL He ain't an awful lookin' iabeck, Bernadette, an' his hair's auburrin.

BERNADETTE Yer taste's in yer mouth, duckie. Anyway . . . eyes off. He's walkin' out with Sarah Morrissy for I seen them meself last Sunday week a-clickin'[117] on the Cab-ar-a Road.[118]

CARMEL Well wait now till I tell ya. He asked me for an A.P.[119] at the Depot[120] next Sunday an' he said to bring a pal an' he'll get her a fella, will ye come?

BERNADETTE Will I come? Te th' Depot? Looka Carmel, I'll be there in me best Viyella.

---

112. "Phibsboro'" Working-class district of Dublin.

113. "Girls' Club" Meeting place for provision shop workers.

114. "Grocers' and Vintners' Assistants Association" Protection association or quasi-union, founded in 1820.

115. "Wet Dreams, Gorgeous Wrecks" For the 1977 editon Johnston accentuated the sexual frankness and violence of rhetoric in the late 1960s, replacing "Dingle's Band and Clarke Barry's" of earlier editions.

116. "iabeck" Dublin slang for idiot or bloke; usually spelled ibex.

117. "a-clickin'" Flirting.

118. "Cab-ar-a" Cabra Road in Cabra, adjacent to Phibsborough in North Dublin.

119. "A.P." Appointment or date.

120. "Depot" Civic Guards Depot.

CARMEL Looka I'm off up to meet him a half five a Doyle's. He said th' Phib, but I think he has one eye on the Courtin' Park if I know that laddo. Do ye know?

BERNADETTE [*giggling*] Ah such gas! Sarah'll be wild when I tell her.

CARMEL That one! You'd think she was someone.

SPEAKER [*politely*] I beg your pardon.

[BERNADETTE *nudges* CARMEL.]

SPEAKER Did I hear you mention Sarah?

BERNADETTE There's a fella tryin' to click.

CARMEL Where? What sort of a fella?

BERNADETTE Behind you. A queer-lookin' skin.

SPEAKER If you would be so good? I'd be very much obliged.

[CARMEL *queries* BERNADETTE *with her eyebrows. The latter thinks not.*]

BERNADETTE Give him the back of yer hand, Carmel. I'm not on.

SPEAKER Could you tell me . . . ?

CARMEL [*turning with great dignity*] Chase yerself Jiggs or I'll call the Guards.[121]

SPEAKER Please don't misunderstand me. I only want to make an inquiry.

[*The two girls look knowingly at one another.*]

BERNADETTE [*in a hoarse whisper*] One of the Foresters.[122]

CARMEL Aw yes, well ye didn't meet me in Bray[123] last summer. So goodbye-ee.

SPEAKER In Bray? I said . . .

[BERNADETTE *giggles hysterically.*]

CARMEL [*to* BERNADETTE] That's th' stuff to give th' trupes.[124] Well, I'll have to be off now or I'll be late. He'll be wild as it is. So long love.

BERNADETTE Corner a Prussia Street a Sunday?

CARMEL Mind yer there a half seven. Ta-ta so.

SPEAKER Listen . . . I must speak. I will not have this!

---

121. "Guards" Police or *Garda Síothchána;* "Pole-iss" in 1932 edition.

122. "Foresters" See note 6.

123. "Bray" Summer resort town south of Dublin and headquarters for Civic Guard in 1920s.

124. "trupes" Troops. From a street ditty: "That's the stuff to give to the troops / Linseed meal and castor oil."

CARMEL Egs-scuse me! But may I ask who you're addressin' in that tone a voice?

BERNADETTE [*fluttering*] Ay—ay!

SPEAKER I can't have this.

[*He tries to restrain her with a hand.*]

BERNADETTE Ay, give us a hand someone!

CARMEL Oh ye can't have this so ye can't, then listen to me, me Mountjoy[125] Masher, ye'll have the flat of me fist across yer puss if ye can't conduct yerself when addressin' a lady, an' I'll thank ye to take that big slab from fingerin' me bawneen[126] before I have ye run in the way God knows ye ought to be pesterin' an' pursuin' a pair a decent girls in th' public thoroughfare!

SPEAKER Stop! For God's sake!

BERNADETTE Ay—ay! Help! Help!

CARMEL It's not safe for a respectable woman to leave th' shadda[127] of her own door, so it's not, for the dirty gowgers[128] that would be after them like . . . [*He tries to place his hand over her mouth. She bites him.* BERNADETTE *screams.*] Looka, I suppose you think yer face is yer fortune, but God knows at that rate some of us should be on the dole!

VOICES Ay, what's up? What's the matter?

CARMEL I declare to God I'd be ashamed of meself. A big lowsey yuck the like of you, why can't ye get a job a honest work and not be annoyin' young girls in th' street. It's lucky for your skin me fella's on th' far side of the Tolka River[129] this minnit d'ye hear that now!

VOICES What did he do?

Is that him?

What's up?

Ay, can't ye leave the girl alone?

[*Rows of heads, hatted and becapped. The Curtains part again, disclosing a street.*]

BERNADETTE [*breathlessly*] Laida—laid aholt of us he did . . . an' says he, didn't I meet you in Bray last summer? says

125. "Mountjoy" Dublin prison on North Circular Road in Dublin district of Phibsborough.
126. "bawneen" *Báinín*, a type of Irish white wool sweater.
127. "shadda" Shadow.
128. "gowgers" Gougers or cheats.
129. "Tolka River" Divides poorer north Dublin from rest of city.

he, didn't I meet you in Bray? . . . An' then he takes her by the arm and says he . . .

SPEAKER I did nothing of the sort!

VOICES Hold that fella.

> Disgusting.
>
> Put him out.

SPEAKER I was only asking the way.

CARMEL [*choking*] Askin' th' way! Now d'ye hear that? . . . only askin' th'—looka what sort of a brass neck has that one got at all!

BERNADETTE Look at what wants to ask th' way!

VOICES [*raucously—laughing*] To ask the way! 'Will any lady show a gentleman how who doesn't know the way?'

AN OLDER MAN Ay, see here now. You ought to know better at your age. You'd better leave the girls alone or maybe some of these days you'll be finding your way where you least expect. This is a decent country.

VOICES Still dear. No longer dirty. [130]

> Keep to the right.
>
> Does your mother know yer out?

SPEAKER

> How shall I reach the land that I love?
>
> Through the way of the wind, the high hills above?
>
> Down by the blue wide ways of the sea?

[*Pause.*]

OLDER MAN What's that?

CARMEL God blessus, he's up the spout!

SPEAKER That this unsparing storm should wreak its wrath . . .

OLDER MAN Ay, give over. What's up with ye?

CARMEL Well ye won't see me in his bewty[131] chorus!

[*General laughter.*]

OLDER MAN Be quiet youse! I'm lookin' after this. What's yer name?

SPEAKER I am Robert Emmet.

A VOICE Robert Emmet?

A VOICE Who?

A VOICE Any relation to Paddy Emmet of Clonakilty?

---

130. "Still dear. No longer dirty." Adaptation from Joyce's headline: "Dear, Dirty Dublin" in Aeolus episode, *Ulysses* 7, line 921.

131. "bewty" Beauty.

OLDER MAN Ssssh!

VOICES Ssssh!

SPEAKER I could explain it all in a moment if only you thought it worth while to give me a chance.

OLDER MAN Oh if you're Robert Emmet you'll get every chance you want here. This is a free country. Is this true what you say?

SPEAKER It is.

BERNADETTE Well, d'ye hear that?

CARMEL Who did he say?

BERNADETTE Emmet. D'ye know. That fella.

A VOICE [as fingers point] That's Robert Emmet.

VOICES Emmet.
Emmet.
That's him.
Ay, d'ye know.

OLDER MAN If yer Robert Emmet it must be all right.

SPEAKER Won't you let me explain?

OLDER MAN You can speak yer mind here without fear or favour.

VOICES Nor sex, nor creed, nor class.[132]
One for all and all for one.
Can laws forbid the blades of grass
From growing as they grow?
That's right.
A free country.
Up freedom!

SPEAKER I knew it would be all right when I told you. And it will be so much better for all of us.

OLDER MAN Let him have his way. I'll see that justice is done.

VOICES Without fear or favour.
That's right.
It's Robert Emmet.
Fair play for all.
Let him have his way.
He's all right.
Be reasonable.

---

132. "without fear or favour. . . . Nor sex, nor creed, nor class." From the "Proclamation of the Republic," read at the Easter Rising of 1916.

Justice.

Free speech.

All right. All right.

OLDER MAN [*fussing round as if putting everybody into their seats*] Sit down now all. Be easy. I'll look after this. I'll see you through. Leave it all to me now an' we'll fix it all up for you in half a jiffy. Isn't that right?

[*General clapping. The* OLDER MAN *assumes an air of platform importance, coughs, and comes forward to address the audience.*]

OLDER MAN Ladies and gents . . . we are very fortunate . . . in having with us tonight . . . one, who . . . I am sure . . . will need no introduction from me to a Dublin audience . . . His fair fame . . . his manly bearing . . . his zeal in the cause of the Gael . . . his upright character . . . his unbounded enthusiasm for the old cause . . . whatever it may or may not have been . . . his Christian charity . . . his wide experience . . . his indefatigable courage . . . his spotless reputation . . . and his kindness to the poor of the city . . . have made his name a household word wherever th' ole flag flies.

CARMEL [*shrilly*] Who wounded Maud McCutcheon?[133]

OLDER MAN [*tolerantly*] Now, now, we mustn't touch on controversial matters . . . In introducing him to you this evening . . . I can say with confidence . . . that you will one and all listen to what he has to say . . . whatever it may be . . . and I am sure we are all looking forward to it very much indeed . . . with the greatest interest and with the deepest respect . . . The views which he has at heart . . . are also very near to the hearts of every one of us in this hall . . . and before calling upon him to address you I would just like to say that the committee will be glad to see any or all of you at the Central Branch Whist Drive in Ierne Hall next Friday and the treasurer will be waiting in the passage as you pass out for those members who have not yet paid their subs. Ladies and gents, Mr—er—er—

A VOICE Emmet.

OLDER MAN Mr Robert Ellis.[134]

[*Applause.*]

SPEAKER Don't gape at me like that. It is you who are confused—not I. It is only in this place that I am mocked. But

133. "Who wounded Maud McCutcheon?" Slogan written on Dublin hoardings in the 1920s, referring to the alleged abuse of a political prisoner.
134. "Mr. Robert Ellis" Traditional name for hangman.

I will carry you away to where the spirit is triumphant . . . where the streets have no terrors and the darkness no babbling torment of voices . . . where all will be plain . . . clear and simple . . . as God's sky above, and the chains will fall from your souls at the first sound of her voice from the lighted window. Which of you would not be free?

BERNADETTE Up the Repubbelick!

SPEAKER We know only one definition of freedom. It is Tone's definition; it is Mitchell's definition; it is Rossa's definition. Let no man blaspheme the cause that the dead generations of Ireland served, by giving it any other name and definition than their name and their definition. Life springs from death, and from the graves of patriot men and women spring living nations. Men and women of Eire, who is with me?[135]

VOICES Up Emmet!
We are with you! Up the Partisans![136]
Fuck a bal la![137] Emmet leads!

SPEAKER But hark, a voice in thunder spake![138] I knew it. Slaves and dastards, stand aside!

VOICES [*with great waving of arms*] Rathfarnham! Rathfarnham!

[*Singing.*]

Yes, Ireland shall be free
From the centre to the sea,
Then hurrah for Liberty!
Says the Shan Van Vocht.

[*Terrific enthusiasm. A queue forms.*]

OLDER MAN [*ringing a hand-bell*] Line up, line up, ladies and gents. This way for Rathfarnham. All aboard for the Priory. Leaving An Lar[139] every three minutes. Plenty of room on top. No waiting. This way ladies and gents. Seats for Rathfarnham.

---

135. "We know only one definition . . . who is with me?" From famous 1915 speech of Patrick Pearse urging revolution at the O'Donovan Rossa Commemoration in Glasnevin Cemetery.

136. "Up the Partisans!" Before 1977 edition, this read: "We are for you!" Johnston admired the single-minded revolutionary tactics of Tito's Partisans, whom he met as a BBC correspondent during World War II. Thereafter he used this term generically to refer to political groups willing to use violent means to achieve their end. See *Nine Rivers from Jordan*, pp. 202–6, 402.

137. "Fuck a bal la!" Before 1977 edition, this read "On, on!" See note 115.

138. "a voice in thunder spake!" Adaptation of "Then spoke the thunder," T. S. Eliot, "The Waste Land," line 399.

139. "*An Lar*" The City Center.

TWO TOUTS [*distributing handbills*] Next bus leaves in ten minutes. All aboard for Tir-na-n'Og.[140] Special reduced return fares at single and a third. The Radio Train for Hy Brasail.[141] No waits. No stops. Courtesy, efficiency and punctuality. Joneses Road, Walsh Road, Philipsburg Avenue, Clontarf, Clonturk,[142] Curran's Cross[143] and the New Jerusalem.

OLDER MAN Now then, quietly, quietly please. There is room for one and all. Step this way please. All those in favour will say 'Taw'.

Put your troubles on the shelf.

Country life restores the health.

[*Many gentlemen and ladies shake hands with the* SPEAKER *as they file past.*]

TWO TOUTS Schoolchildren, under twelve half price. Senior Citizens free. Uniformed social workers will meet young girls travelling alone. Special Whit[144] facilities when not on strike. Penalty for improper use, five pounds. Empyrean[145] Express, Park in Paradise. Hearts' Desire Non-stop picks up and sets down passengers only at the white pole. Please do not spit in or on the conductor.

HANDSHAKERS

Proud to meet you, sir.

Look us up any time you're in Sandymount.

Jacobs Vobiscuits.[146]

The country is with you.

My! how you've grown!

Remember me to the boys.

D'ye vanta vuya vatch?[147]

---

140. "*Tir na n'Og*" In Irish myth, the Land of the Eternally Young; Johnston translated it as "Land of Heart's Desire."

141. See note 10.

142. "Joneses Road . . . Clonturk" Busstops in towns heading northeast from Dublin's *An Lar.*

143. "Curran's Cross" Substitution for Harold's Cross, suburb north of Rathfarnham, where the historical Emmet hid after collapse of his Rebellion.

144. "Whit" Whitsunday or Pentecost, a Catholic sacred feast and Irish holiday.

145. "Empyrean" Highest circle of Paradise, abode of God, in Dante's *Paradiso.*

146. "Jacobs Vobiscuits" Witticism borrowed from *Ulysses* 15, line 1241, in which Joyce conflated a Latin response from the Catholic Mass, *Dominus vobiscum,* with "Jacobs' Biscuit Factory," a Dublin firm. By the time of this play, the allusion had an additional resonance: in the 1916 Rising Thomas MacDonagh turned the Biscuit Factory, which faced Dublin Castle, center of British administration, into a republican fort.

147. "vanta vuya vatch?" Want to buy a watch?

Magnificent, sir!

Would you sign a snap?[148]

Have ye e'er a Green Stamp?

TWO TOUTS Excursions for schools and colleges. Boy Scouts and Girl Guides in uniform admitted free. Tea and boiled eggs may be had from the conductor. Special comfort facilities on all vehicles, except when standing in the station.

[*The queue queues. Presently the* SPEAKER *finds himself shaking hands with the old* FLOWER WOMAN. *There is silence.*]

WOMAN Wait, me love, an' I'll be with ye.

SPEAKER You!

WOMAN I thought I heard th' noise I used to hear when me friends come to visit me.

> Oh, she doesn't paint nor powdher,
> An' her figger-is-all-her-owin.[149]

Hoopsie-daisie! The walk of a Quee-in![150]

SPEAKER Hurry on please.

WOMAN [*patting him roguishly on the shoulder*] Ah, conduct yerself. We're all friends here. Have ye nothing for me, lovely gentleman?

SPEAKER What do you want?

WOMAN It's not food or drink that I want. It's not silver that I want.[151] Ochone.[152]

SPEAKER I have no time to waste talking to you.

WOMAN What is it he called it? . . . the cheapest thing the good God has made . . . eh? He-he-he. That's all. For your own old lady.

SPEAKER I've nothing for you.

WOMAN Gimme me rights . . . me rights first!

SPEAKER Go away!

WOMAN Me rights! Me rights first . . . or I'll bloody well burst ye!

VOICES Get on! Get on!

WOMAN [*turning on the crowd*] Aw ye have a brave haste

---

148. "snap" Photo.

149. "Oh, she doesn't paint . . . owin." "Mike Magilligan's Daughter." *See* note 81.

150. "The walk of a Quee-in" See note 116 of Introduction.

151. "It's not food or drink . . . I want." Yeats's Cathleen asks young Irish men to sacrifice their lives on her behalf in *Cathleen.* See Introduction, p. 39.

152. "Ochone" = alas. A traditional lament.

about ye. Ye have a grand wild spirit to be up an' somewheres, haven't ye! Ye'll be off to a betther land will yez? Ye will . . . in me eye!

VOICES Ah, dry up!

What's she talking about?

Up Emmet!

WOMAN An' a nice lot a bowsy[153] scuts[154] youse are, God knows! Emmet! He-he-he! Up Emmet! Let me tell youse that fella's not at all he says he is!

VOICES What's that? Not Emmet?

WOMAN Look at him, ye gawms![155] Use yer eyes an' ask him for yourselves.

A VOICE But the costume?

WOMAN Five bob a day from Ging.[156]

[*She disappears into the crowd, whispering and pointing.*]

SPEAKER My friends . . .

OLDER MAN Is this true?

SPEAKER My friends . . . we must go on . . . at once.

OLDER MAN I asked you a question.

VOICES Look at him.

Well, what about it?

Perhaps she's right.

SPEAKER We can wait no longer.

VOICES Can't you answer the gentleman's question?

OLDER MAN Are these charges true?

SPEAKER What are you talking about?

YOUNGER MAN [*in a beret*] What's all this?

OLDER MAN This chap says he's Robert Emmet.

SPEAKER I am.

OLDER MAN Oh, you are, are you?

SPEAKER I am.

OLDER MAN Well answer me this then. *What's happened to your boots?*

VOICES Ah-ha!

Look!

What about his boots?

SPEAKER My boots!

---

153. "bowsy" From bowse, a variation of booze.
154. "scuts" Literally, the short upright tail of a deer; here, cowards.
155. "gawms" Gawkers, possibly from "gorms," meaning "stares stupidly."
156. "Ging" Theatre supplies store on Dame Street.

OLDER MAN He comes here an' says he's Robert Emmet, and where are his boots?

VOICES That's right.

Such an idea.

He's an impostor.

Throw him out!

SPEAKER I don't know . . . I thought they were . . . I see your point . . . I . . .

VOICES Well?

SPEAKER Perhaps I had better explain . . . You see . . . someone took them from me when I was playing Robert Emmet and . . .

OLDER MAN [*with heavy sarcasm*] Oh so you were *playing* Robert Emmet? A play-actor are you? Some of this high-brow stuff I suppose?

SPEAKER Oh no, not at all.

VOICES High-brow! Ha!

OLDER MAN I suppose you consider yourself a member of the so-called Intelligentsia? One of the Smart Set.

SPEAKER Me?

VOICES Smart Set! Ha! Ha!

OLDER MAN A self-appointed judge of good taste, eh?

SPEAKER I don't want to judge anything.

VOICES Good taste. Ha! Ha! Ha!

OLDER MAN You want to pose before the world as representative of the Irish people? Eh?

SPEAKER I only want to . . .

VOICES Representative. Ha! Ha! Ha! Ha!

OLDER MAN Tell me [*suddenly*] how much do you get for this?

SPEAKER That's none of your business!

VOICES A job! A job!

He does it for a job!

He's related to someone!

And has a job!

OLDER MAN Honest friends and anti-jobbers! This so-called leader, this self-appointed instructor of the Irish people, is owney linin' his pockets at the expense of the poor. His downy couch, debauched with luxury is watered with the sweat of the humble. A traitor's pillory in the hearts of his countrymen would be a proper reward for such an abattoir of licentiousness.

SPEAKER [*assuming a Parnellesque attitude*] Who is the master of this party?

OLDER MAN Who is the mistress of this party?

SPEAKER Until the party deposes me I am leader.

A VOICE You are not our leader. You are a dirty trickster.

A VOICE Committee Room Fifteen![157]

SPEAKER So you won't follow me any longer?

VOICES No!

SPEAKER [*after a pause*] Very well. I shall just have to go on by myself.

OLDER MAN Oh no you don't. You're not going out of this.

SPEAKER Who's going to stop me?

OLDER MAN We are. You're not going to be allowed to hold up this country to disgrace and ridicule in the eyes of the world. Throwing mud and dirt at the Irish people.[158]

VOICE Give him a taste of backwoodsman's law.[159]

SPEAKER [*to* YOUNGER MAN] Tell him to get out of my way. You won't allow this.

YOUNGER MAN It's nothing to do with me. The army has no interest in civilian affairs. All the same I don't like to see my country insulted by indecent plays.

OLDER MAN That's right.

YOUNGER MAN A high-spirited race resents being held up to scorn before the world, and it shows its resentment [*He takes out a revolver and hands it to the* OLDER MAN.] in various ways. But as I say it has nothing to do with me.

[*He walks away.*]

OLDER MAN [*with revolver*] Take off that uniform.

SPEAKER Put up that revolver. I warn you, I am serious.

[*He stretches out his hand and gently takes it from him. The crowd slowly closes in upon him with sheeplike heedlessness.*]

SPEAKER Stand back or I will have to shoot. I warn you I won't be interfered with, I am going on at all costs.

157. "Who is the master of this party? . . . Committee Room Fifteen!" In this room in 1890, the majority of the Irish Party in British Parliament deposed Parnell, their leader in the fight for Home Rule, after revelation of his adulterous relationship with Mrs. Katharine O'Shea.

158. "Throwing mud and dirt at the Irish people" Reference to the riots at, and published denunciations of, the Abbey productions of J. M. Synge's *The Playboy of the Western World* (1907) and Sean O'Casey's *The Plough and the Stars* (1926). Johnston hoped his own play would cause a similar uproar.

159. "backwoodsman's law" Vigilante action.

VOICES Traitor. Spy. Cheat. Cur.

SPEAKER [*hidden in their midst*] Back! Back! Slaves and dastards, stand aside! Back! Back! or I'll . . .

[*The revolver emits a dull pop. The crowd melts away to the side and he is disclosed standing there alone with the smoking weapon still clenched in his fist. There is a deathlike silence.*]

A VOICE Oh, my God!

OLDER MAN [*very quietly*] Now you've done it.

SPEAKER Done what?

OLDER MAN You've plugged somebody.

A VOICE Oh, my God! My God!

SPEAKER I've what?

A MAN [*looking out*] It's Joe.

SECOND MAN Joe?

FIRST MAN He's got it in the breast.

YOUNGER MAN [*reappearing*] Who fired that shot?

OLDER MAN Joe's got it. Right through the left lung. He can't last long.

SECOND MAN Christ!

FIRST MAN It wasn't any of us, Tom. It was this chap.

SPEAKER Stand back, stand back, I tell you. I'm fighting. This is war.

YOUNGER MAN [*quite unperturbed*] There's a man out there. You've put a bullet through his breast.

OLDER MAN God rest his soul!

SPEAKER I warned you—I warned you all.

YOUNGER MAN He's going to die. You did it. That's what comes of having guns.

VOICES He's going to die.
　　　You did it.
　　　You did it.

SPEAKER I had to. It wasn't my gun.

[*Two men appear bearing between them the body of another. The people take off their hats and stand mutely with bowed heads.*]

JOE It's welling out over me shirt, boys . . . Can't anybody stop . . . it?

YOUNGER MAN A good man . . . a true man . . . That is what you did.

OLDER MAN That is what he did.

VOICES You did.
　　　He did.

Robert Emmet did.
Who did it?
He did it.
He there.

SPEAKER I had to . . . [*All hands point.*]

JOE Give me . . . me beads[160] . . . before the life . . . has ebbed out of me . . . I can't breathe . . . oh, lads, I'm going . . .

SPEAKER What could I do? I ask you, what could I do? It was war. I didn't mean to hurt him.

OLDER MAN Joe, old scout. We're sorry . . . we're . . . O God!

JOE God bless you boys . . . sure I know . . . I know well . . . it wasn't any of . . . you . . .

SPEAKER [*flinging down the revolver*] Shoot back then! It is war. Shoot! I can die too!

YOUNGER MAN Will that give him back the warm blood you have stolen from him?

OLDER MAN Ah, leave him alone, Tom, leave him alone.

VOICES [*whispering*] Leave him alone.
He shot Joe.
Through the breast.
Poor Joe.
Leave him alone.

JOE [*as he is carried off, followed by the crowd*] O my God . . . I am heartily . . . sorry . . . for having offended . . . Thee . . . and . . . I . . .[161]

VOICES [*chanting*] *Lacrymosa dies illa*
Qua resurget ex favilla
Judicandus homo reus.
Huic ergo parce Deus;
Pie Jesu Domine
Dona eis requiem
Amen.[162]

FLOWER WOMAN [*appearing in the shadows, but speaking with the voice of SARAH CURRAN*]

---

160. "me beads" My rosary. This scene imitates Johnny's execution in O'Casey's *Juno and the Paycock*, act 3.

161. "O my God . . . I . . . " Catholic Act of Contrition, a formal prayer said as part of Confession ritual.

162. "*Lacrymosa dies illa . . . Amen.*" From the "Dies Irae" hymn in the Catholic Mass for the Dead.

Do not make a great keening
When the graves have been dug tomorrow.
Do not call the white-scarfed riders
To the burying . . .[163]

[*Hoarsely*] Ay misther—spare a copper for a cuppa tea—spare a copper for a poor old lady—a cuppa tea—[*Whisper.*] a copper for your own ole lady, lovely gentleman.

[*She fades away.*]

SPEAKER Sally! Sally!—where are you?—where are you? Sally!

THE CURTAIN FALLS

163. "Do not make . . . To the burying" From Yeats's *Cathleen ni Houlihan*, p. 85.

PART TWO

[*Through the Curtain, admidst a hearty round of applause, comes the* MINISTER's *talented daughter,* MAEVE.[164] *She has on a nice white dress with a white bow to match in her long, loose, black hair which reaches quite to her waist. Around her neck on a simple gold chain hangs a religious medal. She curtsies in charming embarrassment and commences to recite.*]

MAEVE Kingth Bweakfatht.[165]
      The King athed de Queen
      And de Queen athed de Dar-med
      Could—I [*a little breathlessly*]—se—butter
      For-de-roy———thlaice—a—bwead?
      Queen athed de Dar-med
      De Dar-med thed Thertinley
      Ah goan tell—Cow now
      For he goeth tebed . . .

[*She continues this amusing piece to the very end, when the Curtain parts amid general applause disclosing a fantastically respectable drawing-room loud with the clatter of tea things. A party is in progress under the aegis of the* MINISTER FOR ARTS AND CRAFTS *and his nice little* WIFE. *The guests consist of one of the* REDCOATS, *now a* GENERAL *in a green uniform, the Statue of* GRATTAN, *rather a nice woman called* LADY TRIMMER[166]— *one of those people whose expression of pleased expectancy never for a moment varies, the old* FLOWER WOMAN *who is seated unobtrusively in the background eating an orange, and a small but enthusi-*

---

164. "Maeve" Queen of Connacht in the ancient Irish epic, the *Táin*.
165. "Kingth Bweakfatht" "The King's Breakfast," *When We Were Very Young,* first published by A. A. Milne in 1924.
166. See note 10 of Introduction.

astic CHORUS. *Side by side upon the sofa reading from right to left are* O'COONEY[167] *the well-known dramatist,* O'MOONEY[168] *the rising portrait painter, and* O'ROONEY[169] *the famous novelist.* O'COONEY *wears a cloth cap, blue sweater and a tweed coat.* O'MOONEY *has a red shirt and horn-rimmed spectacles, while* O'ROONEY *is dressed in full saffron kilt together with Russian boots. The* MINISTER *himself bears a strange resemblance to the* STAGE HAND. *It is all very nice indeed.*]

CHORUS
Oh very nice nice
Oh very nice nice nice
How old how nice how very nice don't you think so
Oh yes indeed yes very nice indeed I do think so indeed don't you indeed.

[*Teaspoons clink.*]

LADY TRIMMER What was that one, my dear?

MAEVE Kingth Bweakfatht pleathe.

LADY TRIMMER Very nice indeed, Maeve. I must teach that one to my two chicks. Where do you learn, my dear?

MAEVE The Banba Thcool of Acting, Lower Abbey Thweet.

CHORUS The Banba School of Acting, Lower Abbey Street.

O'COONEY Wasn't that bloody awful?

O'MOONEY The question is, is she an aartist? A real aartist?

O'ROONEY O'Mooney sounds better with his mouth shut.

WIFE Of course, she hasn't been learning very long. But she has the language, and that's half the battle these days. Show them, Maeve.

MAEVE *Céad míle fáilte.*[170]

LADY TRIMMER Oh very good indeed. But of course, she has her father's talent.

---

167. "O'Cooney" Sean O'Casey.

168. "O'Mooney" Patrick Tuohy, painter of James Joyce's portrait in 1924, and so the subject of begrudging admiration among Dublin's young avant-garde for whom Joyce was the symbol of rebellion against Dublin's orthodoxies. See note 191.

169. "O'Rooney" Liam O'Flaherty, author of a number of famous Irish novels including *The Informer* (1925). Anxious to prevent a narrow Irish nationalism, he was leader of a party of workers who in 1922 declared a short-lived Soviet Irish Republic.

170. "*Céad míle fáilte*" A hundred thousand welcomes.

MINISTER Ah, well, now . . .

WIFE [*pleased*] Oh, Lady Trimmer!

MINISTER Well, now, all the same I don't know about that. But mind you I do say this, Talent is what the country wants. Politics may be all O.K. in their way, but what I say to *An Taoiseach*[171] is this, until we have Talent and Art in the country we have no National Dignity. We must have Talent and Art. Isn't that right?

CHORUS We must have Art have Talent and Art.

LADY TRIMMER Quite. And cultivated people of taste. You musn't forget them, Mr Minister. Art cannot live you know by taking in its own washing—if I may put it that way.

O'COONEY Aw Holy God!

O'MOONEY [*ruminatively*] The reel aartist must be fundamental. Like Beethoven. Now, *I'm* fundamental.

O'ROONEY Fundament,[172] all right.

MINISTER Now see here. I'm Minister for Arts and Crafts, you see. Well, a young fellow comes along to me and he says, Now look, Liam, here's some Art I'm after doing . . . it might be a book you see, or a drawing, or even a poem . . . and can you do anything for me, he says? Well, with that, I do . . . if he deserves it, mind you, only if he deserves it, under Section 15 of the Deserving Artists' (Support) Act, No. 65 of 1926.[173] And there's none of this favouritism at all.

CHORUS The State supports the Artist.

GRATTAN And the Artist supports the State.

CHORUS Very satisfactory for everybody and no favouritism at all.

MINISTER [*confidentially*] And of course, then you see, it helps us to keep an eye on the sort of stuff that's turned out, you understand.

CHORUS Clean and pure Art for clean and pure people.

LADY TRIMMER What we need most is a small Salon.

GENERAL That's right. A small Art Saloon.

WIFE We often have people in on Sunday evenings for music and things. Won't you sing something now, General?

171. "*An Taoiseach*" The chief, title of Irish prime minister.
172. "Fundament" Excrement.
173. "Section 15 . . . No. 65 of 1926" The Irish Free State moved immediately to control the media, passing in 1923 a Censorship of Film Act "to protect the youth of the country," and in 1929 a Censorship of Publications Act.

GENERAL Aw, I have no voice at all.

O'COONEY He's bloody well right there.

O'MOONEY The question is . . . Is he fundamental?

LADY TRIMMER Just somewhere where the nicest people . . . the people one wants to meet . . . like Mr O'Cooney and Mr O'Mooney . . .

O'ROONEY [*suspiciously*] And Mr O'Rooney.

LADY TRIMMER *And* Mr O'Rooney, can get together quietly and discuss Art and common interests.

WIFE Haven't you brought your music?

CHORUS You must have brought your music.

GENERAL Well now . . . if you insist. Maybe I might find something.

O'COONEY [*to* O'MOONEY] Ay, have *you* put my cap somewhere?

WIFE Do, General.

GENERAL I don't know for sure, mind you. I might . . . just happen to have something on me.

[*He produces a roll of music from inside his tunic.*]

CHORUS The General's going to sing.

GENERAL Ah, but . . . sure there's no one to play th' accompanyment.

WIFE Maeve will play. Won't you, darling?

MAEVE Yeth mammy.

[*Signs of distress from the sofa.*]

WIFE Of course you will dear. Give her the music, General.

CHORUS Ssssh!

[*The* GENERAL *gives her the music rather doubtfully and they are opening the peformance, when there comes a loud, peremptory knock at the door. General surprise.*]

WIFE [*bravely but apprehensively*] What can that be?

LADY TRIMMER Strange!

MINISTER A knock at the door?

GENERAL Ah now, isn't that too bad!

CARMEL [*entering*] There's a gentleman at the door, ma'am, looking for the Rathfarnham bus.

WIFE What kind of a gentleman, Carmel?

CARMEL A gentleman in a uniform, ma'am.

MINISTER A uniform? Tell me, does he look like the start of a Daring Outrage?

CHORUS Possibly the Garda Síothchána.[174]

CARMEL He has a sword, sir.

MINISTER A sword?

CARMEL [*primly*] And a pair of slippers.

WIFE Slippers?

GENERAL I don't think I know that unyform.

CHORUS Can't be the Garda Síothchána after all.

WIFE Did he give any name, Carmel?

CARMEL Yes, ma'am. A Mr Emmet.

LADY TRIMMER Not *the* Mr Emmet?

CARMEL I don't know I'm sure, ma'am.

MINISTER Ah, yes I remember. That's him all right.

GENERAL Aw, the hard Emmet.

MINISTER The old Scout.

WIFE The gentleman who is far from the land. Show him up at once, Carmel.

CARMEL Yes, ma'am. [*She goes, muttering.*] Doesn't look like a sailor to me.

LADY TRIMMER How nice of him to call.

WIFE Yes, indeed, but you know we can't be too careful since the Trouble.[175]

MINISTER Emmet's all right. I know him well. Used to work with him in the old days.

GENERAL Aw, the rare old Emmet.

LADY TRIMMER You know I've wanted to meet him for such a long time. My husband always says that we of the old regime ought to get into touch with those sort of people as much as possible. We can assist each other in so many ways.

MINISTER That's right. We must all get together for the good of the country.

WIFE I wonder has he brought his music too?

GRATTAN I expect he has.

[CARMEL *enters, cocking her head contemptuously towards the* SPEAKER, *who follows her with a strange, hunted look in his eye. He glances round apprehensively as though prepared for the worst and yet hoping against hope.*]

---

174. "*Garda Síothchána*" Guardians of the peace, name of the Dublin police force.

175. "the Trouble" Euphemism, usually in the plural, for the time of the Anglo-Irish War (1919–21) and the Civil War (1922–23), and still used to describe Ireland's continuing strife.

CHORUS Oh how do you how do you how do you how do you how . . .

WIFE How do you do? Bring another cup, Carmel.

CARMEL Yes, ma'am. [*She goes, muttering.*] I'll have to wash one first.[176]

SPEAKER Excuse . . . me.

WIFE Come and sit down and let me introduce you to everybody. It was so nice of you to call. Liam has just been speaking about your work.

SPEAKER I only came in to ask . . .

CHORUS Have you brought your music?

WIFE This is Lady Trimmer, Mr Emmet.

CHORUS Of the old regime.

LADY TRIMMER Dee do.

SPEAKER [*after peering closely into her face*] No, ah, no.

LADY TRIMMER You must come and visit us too, Mr Emmet. First Fridays. Now promise.

WIFE And General O'Gowna[177] of the *Oglaigh na h-Eireann*.[178]

GENERAL [*affably*] And many of them.

SPEAKER It was you who hit me.

WIFE And of course you know my husband, the Minister for Arts and Crafts.

CHORUS Vote *Fianna na Poblacht*.[179]

MINISTER *A chara*.[180]

[*The SPEAKER tries to remonstrate but is hurried on.*]

WIFE And Mr Grattan's statue from College Green.

GRATTAN Welcome Don Quixote Alighieri.[181] Did I speak the truth?

[*The SPEAKER's head goes up.*]

WIFE And this is Mr O'Cooney, the great dramatist.

176. "I'll have to wash one first." Carmel's dirty cup routine first appears in 1977 edition, Johnston's comment on the changed class relations in modern Dublin.

177. "O'Gowna" In notebook draft, he was Smith but changed his name to O'Smidda to acquire requisite Irishness for the new Free State.

178. "*Oglaigh na h-Eireann*" Young Men of Ireland, name of the Irish volunteers, the post-1917 Irish Republican Army.

179. "*Fianna na Poblacht*" Fenian soldiers or physical force Republicans in Civil War and the nucleus of the Fianna Fáil political party led by Eamon de Valera, who was elected *Taoiseach* of the Free State in 1932.

180. "*A chara*" = friend.

181. "Don Quixote Alighieri" Conflation of Cervantes' Don Quixote, and Dante Alighieri, author and hero of *Divine Comedy*.

SPEAKER Cap?

WIFE Oh, Mr O'Cooney always wears his cap in the drawing-room.

O'COONEY And why the bloody hell shouldn't I wear my cap in the drawing-room?

[*General laughter.*]

SPEAKER I see.

O'MOONEY Now me.

WIFE This is Mr O'Mooney, the artist, if you can remember everybody.

O'MOONEY The reel Aartist.

O'COONEY The owl cod.

WIFE Oh, please, Mr O'Cooney!

CHORUS I love the way he talks, don't you?

O'MOONEY Oh, don't mind O'Cooney. He's a great friend of mine, really.

O'COONEY He is not!

WIFE And this is Mr O'Rooney, the well-known novelist. Now I think you know everybody.

SPEAKER [*indicating the costume*] You play the pipes?

[O'MOONEY *laughs shrilly.*]

O'ROONEY I do not. I do not believe in political Nationalism. Do you not see my Russian boots?

WIFE Mr O'Rooney believes in the workers.

O'ROONEY I do not believe in the workers. Nor do I believe in the Upper Classes nor in the Bourgeoisie. It should be perfectly clear by now what I do not believe in, unless you wish me to go over it again?

LADY TRIMMER [*archly*] Mr O'Rooney, you dreadful man!

SPEAKER I'm sorry.

WIFE Sit down now and have a nice cup of tea.

[CARMEL *meanwhile has been back with a dirty cup.*]

CHORUS I do like a nice cup of tea.

SPEAKER So she is here, too!

WIFE What's that?

SPEAKER That damned old flower woman who turned them all against me!

WOMAN Ay, mister, have ye e'er an old hempen rope for a neckcloth?

WIFE You're joking, Mr Emmet. There's no old flower woman.

SPEAKER I mean . . . look there.

WIFE Have some tea, Mr Emmet. You're a little tired, no doubt.

SEMICHORUS Delightful drink.

SEMICHORUS Pity it tans the stomach.

WIFE You'll feel much the better of it. And we'll have a little music afterwards. We often have music in the evenings.

MINISTER Are you interested in Art, Mr Emmet?

LADY TRIMMER I suppose you're a member of the Nine Arts Club?

WIFE And the Royal Automobile Academy?

CHORUS Celebrity Concerts.[182] The Literary Literaries.

SPEAKER I don't feel very . . . Did you say that statue of Grattan was there?

WIFE Oh yes, that's Mr Grattan's statue from College Green. We always have a few of the nicest statues in on Sunday evening. My husband is Minister for Arts and Crafts, you know.

LADY TRIMMER Just to form a little group you know. A few people of taste.

WIFE Of course we're only amateurs, but we're doing our best.

[Pause.]

SPEAKER [suddenly] Let me be persuaded that my springing soul may meet the . . .

[Pause.]

LADY TRIMMER I beg your pardon?

SPEAKER Let me be per—[He shakes his head hopelessly.] I am Robert Emmet.

GRATTAN You are not.

SPEAKER Who are you to question me?

GRATTAN You are only a play-actor.

SPEAKER Look well to your own soul, Major Sirr!

GRATTAN Have you found your Holy Curran, Galahad?[183]

WIFE I always say to Liam, Liam you really *must* get a proper statue of Mr Emmet. It's positively disgraceful that we haven't got a good one, don't you think?

---

182. "Nine Arts . . . Celebrity Concerts" Dublin social clubs of the 1920s.

183. "Galahad" The Arthurian hero whose spiritual perfection was rewarded in his quest for the Holy Grail.

MINISTER Ah, well, dear, you know, expense, expense.

LADY TRIMMER What a nice uniform! Tell me, do you admire the plays of Chekhov?

WIFE Perhaps he acts for the Civil Service Dramatics.[184]

SPEAKER Act? . . . No. No cake, thank you.

CHORUS Benevente Strindberg Toller Euripides Pirandello Tolstoy Calderon O'Neill.[185]

LADY TRIMMER I'm sure you'd be good.

CHORUS An annual subscription of one guinea admits a member to all productions and to all At Homes.

MINISTER [*confidentially*] Say the word and I'll get you into the Rathmines and Rathmines.[186] I know the man below.

LADY TRIMMER Now do tell us, Mr Emmet, about your wonderful experiences in the Trouble.

[*The* SPEAKER *spills his tea and looks around wild-eyed.*]

SPEAKER What do you mean?

GRATTAN Ah—ha!

WIFE Never mind. It's quite all right. I'll pour you out another cup.

LADY TRIMMER [*hastily*] You must have had such interesting times all through the fighting.

SPEAKER I shall never fight again!

[*He buries his face in his hands.*]

MINISTER Oh come, Mr Emmet! What's the matter?

WIFE Are you not feeling well?

LADY TRIMMER [*aside*] Ssssh! Don't pay any attention. I understand. Do tell us about it, Mr Emmet. Talk. Talk someone.

SPEAKER God have pity on me.

CHORUS Oh the fighting everyone talk don't pay any attention wonderful experiences those were the attention fighting days how wonderful do tell us about the fighting days interesting and wonderful.

SPEAKER It was I who shot him and you all know it! You all know! Isn't it enough for you? Haven't I suffered enough?

CHORUS [*louder*] Oh tuttut poor man don't talk do talk

---

184. "Civil Service Dramatics" Amateur theatre group of 1920s.

185. "Chekhov . . . O'Neill" Dramatists whose plays were produced by Johnston and other amateurs in the 1920s. See Introduction, pp. 9–11.

186. "Rathmines and Rathmines" Added in 1960 edition, mocking the popular Amateur theatre group, "Rathmines and Rathgar."

as hard as you can fighting wonderful pay no attention shellshock probably to have seen it all wonderful is he better yet poor man everybody pretend not to fighting notice.

SPEAKER They trapped me! A good man . . . a true man . . . and I did it!

WIFE Well what if you did shoot somebody? Everybody's shot somebody nowadays. That'll soon be over.[187]

LADY TRIMMER Yes, yes; of course we didn't approve of it at the time, but it's all so interesting now.

SPEAKER Interesting!

CHORUS Perhaps we had better how is he change the subject change the subject getting on what's the wonderful experiences matter with him matter with him at all?

WIFE How about a little song?

CHORUS How about a little little song song song?

WIFE Do you sing, Mr Emmet?

SPEAKER What do you all want with me?

LADY TRIMMER Nothing, nothing at all, Mr Emmet. Perhaps you'd like to act us a little snippet from your play?

WIFE We often have plays on Sunday evenings. Poor man. There, there. We are all friends here.

LADY TRIMMER The General has just obliged us.

GENERAL I have not. I was interrupted before I got going.

WIFE You're better now, I'm sure. Of course you are. Aren't you?

MINISTER Well, I believe in supporting Art and acting's Art. So you have *my* consent anyhow.

WIFE You'll act something for us, Mr Emmet, won't you?

GRATTAN Ah, leave him alone. Can't you see he's beaten.

SPEAKER That voice! That voice!

GRATTAN I said that you were beaten. You should have taken my advice from the first; but you would go on with your play-acting. Now, perhaps you know better. Rathfarnham! Ha! Sarah Curran! Ha-ha-ha!

SPEAKER [*slowly rising*] I am not beaten. I still believe. I will go on.

CHORUS Oh good, he's going to do something for us.

WIFE Oh do, Mr Emmet.

---

187. "That'll soon be over." Previous to 1977 edition, this read: "That's all over now."

GENERAL But look here . . .

GRATTAN Don't be a fool. Do you imagine that they'll listen to you if you do?

MINISTER Nothing political. That's barred of course.

O'COONEY For God's sake make it short anyhow.

O'MOONEY Nothing Iberian. There's no Iberian real Art.

O'ROONEY See that it's not pompous. That would be an insult to the people of this country.

GENERAL Hey, what about my song?

GRATTAN Go on. Tell them all to go to hell.

SPEAKER Please, please . . . if you want me to do it . . .

CHORUS Oh yes yes, do Mr Emmet.

MINISTER I suppose it will be all right. I wouldn't like anything by somebody with the slave mind, you know.

SPEAKER Nobody can object to my play.

MINISTER Or calculated to excite you-know-what.

CHORUS Emmet's play is all right.

GENERAL Well you needn't expect me to sit down quietly under this sort of behaviour. When you ask a man to sing . . .

SPEAKER [advancing towards the audience] It's very hard without Sally. It may seem a little strange here . . . but I'll do it.

GRATTAN Very well. Have it your own way.

LADY TRIMMER Did I hear him mention somebody called . . . er, Sally Somebody?

WIFE [confidentially] I think it must be his young lady.

LADY TRIMMER How charming.

GENERAL [determinedly] One of Moore's Melodies entitled 'She is Far from the Land'.

[He bows.]

O'COONEY Aw, this'll be bloody awful. [Settles down.] D'ye remember that night, Liam, when the two of us hid in the chimbley from the Tans?

MINISTER Will I ever forget it? Ah, those were the days, Seamus.

SPEAKER I had got to the part where I am arrested, hadn't I? No. I think I was . . .

WIFE We always have music and things on Sunday evenings.

LADY TRIMMER Just a nucleus. A few nice people.

GENERAL [*to* MAEVE] Have you got the place?

MAEVE Mammy.

WIFE Yes, dear?

MAEVE Why ith that man wearing hith thlipperth in the dwawing woom?

WIFE Hush, dear, you mustn't ask questions. You must be a good girl.

MAEVE [*plaintively*] You never let me—

GENERAL Ah, go on when I tell you!

[MAEVE *commences the introduction to* 'She is Far from the Land'.]

SPEAKER

The air is rich and soft—the air is mild and bland.

Her woods are tall and straight, grove rising over grove.

Trees flourish in her glens below and on her heights above,

Oh, the fair hills of Eire, oh.

O'ROONEY Will you move up on the sofa and breathe into yourself.

O'MOONEY We'd be better off if your hips were as soft as your head.

[*Simultaneously.*]

SPEAKER	GENERAL [*singing*]
Down from the high cliffs the rivulet is teeming	She is far from the land where her young hero sleeps
To wind around the willow banks that lure me from above;	And lovers around her are sighing:
Ah, where the woodbines with sleepy arms have wound me.	But coldly she turns from their gaze and weeps For her heart in his grave is lying.

MINISTER [*solo*] And do you remember the day, Seamus, of the big round-up in Moore Street when the 'G' man[188] tried to plug me getting out of the skylight?

SPEAKER, GENERAL, and O'COONEY [*simultaneously*]

SPEAKER [*louder*]	GENERAL
But there is lightning in my blood; red lightning tightening in my blood. Oh! if there was a sword in every Irish	She sings the wild songs of her dear native plains, Every note which he loved awaking.

188. "G'man" Gunman.

hand! If there was a flame in
every Irish heart to put an
end to slavery and shame!
Oh, I would end these things!

Ah! little they think, who
delight in her strains,
How the heart of the ministrel
is breaking.

O'COONEY

Aw, Jesus, and the evenings down in the old I.R.B.[189]
in Talbot Street, picking out the 'Soldiers' Song' on
the blackboard.

SPEAKER, MINISTER, and GENERAL [simultaneously]

I have written my name in
letters of fire across the page
of history. I have unfurled the
green flag in the streets and
cried aloud from the high
places to the people of the
Five Kingdoms: Men of Eire,
awake to be blest! to be blest!

He had lived for his love, for
his country he died,
They were all that to life had
entwined him;
Nor soon shall the tears of his
country be dried,
Nor long will his love stay
behind him.

MINISTER

Sometimes I wish I was back again on the run with
the old flying column[190] out by the Glen of Aherlow.
[O'MOONEY and O'ROONEY join in in low under-
tones.]

O'ROONEY

My good woman, I said, I'll
tell you what's wrong with
you. Virginity, my good
woman, that's all. And
believe me, its nothing to be
proud of.

O'MOONEY

Saint Peetric d'ye see because
Saint Peter was the rock and
Saint Patrick was the seed.
That makes Saint Peetric,
d'ye see. For the rock is
underneath and the seed lies
above, so Saint Peter and
Saint Patrick are Saint
Peetric.[191]

189. "I.R.B." Irish Republican Brotherhood, reformed by 1910 as a private
army with Patrick Pearse as one of the leaders; nucleus of the rebels who fought to
create an Irish Republic by means of the 1916 Rising.

190. "flying column" Irish guerrilla fighters.

191. "Saint Peetric" In his 17 March 1927 diary entry, Johnston reports on the
Nine Arts Ball: "Tuohy drunk and talking endlessly of . . . the prose form of Joyce's
coming Anna Livia—'Sayint Peetrick d'ye know—Sayint Peetrick because Sayint Pether
was the rock and Sayint Patrick the seed—Sayint Peetrick, d'ye see?' And Liam O'Flaherty in slippers and nattily-cut tweeds, charming the ladies politely . . . " (Record,
pp. 165–66).

[*At the same time.*]

O'COONEY

And that night waiting up on the North Circular[192]
for word of the executions.[193] Ah, not for all the
wealth of the world would I give up the maddenin'
minglin' memories of the past . . . [194]

SPEAKER   GENERAL

Rise, Arch of the Ocean and
Queen of the West! I have
dared all for Ireland, I will
dare all again for Sarah   O! make her a grave where the
Curran. Their graves are red.   sunbeams rest
O make her a maddening   When they promise a glorious
mingling glorious morrow . . .   morrow . . .

[*The black curtain closes behind the* SPEAKER, *blotting out
the room, and the voices fade away. The* SPEAKER *himself has
somehow chimed in upon the last few lines of the song, and is left
singing it by himself.*]

SPEAKER

They'll shine o'er her sleep like a smile from the west,
From her own loved island of sorrow . . .

[*The* BLIND MAN *comes tap-tapping with a fiddle under his
arm and a tin mug in his hand. He bumps lightly into the* SPEAKER.]

BLIND MAN [*feeling with his stick*] Peek-a-boo! Peek-a-
boo!

SPEAKER Damn your eyes!

BLIND MAN [*looking up*] That's right.

SPEAKER You're . . . blind?

BLIND MAN [*with a chuckle*] That's what they say.

SPEAKER I didn't know. I didn't mean to hurt you.

BLIND MAN Ah, not at all. I'm not so easy hurted. [*Feeling him over.*] Oh, a grand man. A grand man. A grand man
surely, from the feel of his coat.

SPEAKER Do you know where I am?

BLIND MAN Well, isn't that a rare notion now! Asking

---

192. "North Circular" See note 125.
193. "executions" Fifteen of the ninety Irish rebels captured in the 1916 Rising
were executed by the British, an act that created Irish support for the rebels' cause.
194. "D'ye remember that night . . . minglin' memories of the past." O'Cooney's and the General's reminiscences drawn from characterizations of Captain Boyle
and his crony, Joxer Daly, in Sean O'Casey's *Juno and the Paycock.*

the way of an old dark fiddler,[195] and him tip-tappin' over the cold sets[196] day in and day out with never sight nor sign of the blessed sun above.

SPEAKER I give it up.

BLIND MAN And where might you be bound for, stranger?

SPEAKER The Priory.

BLIND MAN [*with a start*] Ah, so! So you're bound for them parts, are you, stranger dear?

SPEAKER Yes.

BLIND MAN Up the glen maybe as far as the edge of the white mist, and it hanging soft around the stones of Mount Venus,[197] eh stranger? He-he-he!

SPEAKER That's right.

BLIND MAN Oh, I know you. I know you. Sure all the Queer Ones[198] of the twelve counties do be trysting around them hills beyond the Priory.

SPEAKER The blessed hills!

BLIND MAN It's sad I am, stranger, for my light words of greeting and the two of us meeting for the first time. Take my arm now, and walk with me for a while and I'll put you on your way. Come—take my arm! Why should you not take my arm, stranger, for I'm telling you, my fathers are Kings in Thomond[199] so they are.

SPEAKER [*taking his arm gingerly*] There.

BLIND MAN That's better now. He-he-he. 'Tis proud I am to be walking arm in arm with the likes of you, stranger. Tell me now, or am I wrong? Would you by any chance be Mr Robert Emmet?

SPEAKER You know me?

BLIND MAN Uh! I thought I recognized them words I heard you singing.

SPEAKER Yes. I am Robert Emmet. He said that I wasn't. But I am. It was the voice of Major Sirr.

---

195. "Asking the way of an old dark fiddler" This character modelled, in part, on J. M. Synge's Martin Doul in *The Well of the Saints*. See Introduction, pp. 39–40.

196. "sets" Pavement stones.

197. "Mount Venus" Huge megalithic Cromlech in County Dublin. In Mary Manning's novel, *Mount Venus,* this is a gathering spot for Maud Gonne and other revolutionaries.

198. "all the Queer Ones" Possibly referring to executed prisoners.

199. "Kings in Thomond" Descendents of Brian Boru, king of Ireland who, although mortally wounded in battle at Clontarf in 1014, broke the power of the Vikings.

BLIND MAN Ah, poor Bob Emmet. He died for Ireland. God rest his soul.

SPEAKER He died. I died?

BLIND MAN You did indeed. You remember the old song we used to sing?

[*They sit down together.*]

SPEAKER You mean 'The Struggle is Over'.

BLIND MAN That's right. Ah, the rare old lilt of it. How does it go, now? [*He sings.*]

The struggle is over, our boys are defeated,
  And Erin surrounded with silence and gloom.
We were betrayed and shamefully treated
  And I, Robert Emmet, awaiting my doom.
Hanged, drawn and quartered, sure that was my sentence,
  But soon I will show them, no coward am I.
My crime was the love of the land I was born in.
  A hero I've lived and a hero I'll die.

BOTH
    Bold Robert Emmet, the darling of Erin,
    Bold Robert Emmet will die with a smile.
    Farewell companions, both loyal and daring,
    I'll lay down my life for the Emerald Isle.

[*Pause. From somewhere comes faint dance music.*]

BLIND MAN Ah, them are the songs. Them are the songs.

SPEAKER He died for Ireland. I died. I?

BLIND MAN High Kings in Thomond, my fathers are. Lords of the Gael. You'll know them, stranger.

SPEAKER How can I have died for Ireland? What is that I hear?

BLIND MAN Ah, never mind that. That's nothing. Nothing at all.

[*A young man in evening dress and a pretty girl are walking out of the darkness into the edge of the light. It is the* TRINITY MEDICAL *and his friend, now a little older. They are smoking and laughing together.*]

SPEAKER Go away.

BLIND MAN Never heed them stranger. That's nobody at all.

SPEAKER And I am dead this hundred years and more?

BLIND MAN What would the likes of you have to do with the likes of them? He-he-he.

HE I remember when I was a kid in Clyde Road[200] how wonderful I thought a private dance was.

SHE Now I suppose you've quite grown out of us all.

HE [*laughing*] Oh, well, I wouldn't say that. But of course when one's lived abroad things do seem a little different, when you come back.

SHE I suppose so.

HE Small in a way and rather provincial. But that's to be expected.

SPEAKER I wonder is Sally dead too?

BLIND MAN Dust to dust and ashes to ashes.

HE Of course, there have been a lot of improvements. But over there . . . well, after all, it takes over an hour and a half to get into the country.

SHE And you like that?

HE Well, you know how it is. It makes one feel one's sort of *in* the world. Everything seems more serious, somehow.

SHE While we and the old days never seemed serious at all.

HE Oh well, I didn't quite mean it that way.

SPEAKER O God help me!

BLIND MAN Coming and going on the mailboat.[201] And they thinking themselves the real ones—the strong ones! I do have to laugh sometimes and I hearing the wings of the Queer Ones beating under the arch of the sky.

HE Of course I liked the old days. We had some jolly good times together, didn't we?

SHE I liked them too.

HE I was crazy about you.

SHE My eye and Betty Martin.

HE I was. I was, really. I often think about it all. It's a bit lonely sometimes over there, and often—Oh, I don't know. Do you ever think about me?

SHE Sometimes.

HE I hope you do. You know, Daphne, sometimes I wonder whether you and I oughtn't to have . . .

SHE Have what?

HE I think we ought to have . . . maybe we still could . . .

---

200. "Clyde Road" Fashionable address in Ballsbridge.
201. "mailboat" Passenger boat from Dún Laoghaire to England.

[*The music stops. There is a pause.*]

HE Hello. The music's stopped.

SHE Yes. I suppose it has.

HE Like to go in and have a drink?

SHE I think we might as well.

HE [*briskly*] Funny, you know, how the old place can get you for a bit. But after all, one can't get away from the fact that it's all so damned depressing—[*They vanish.*]

SPEAKER O God, make speed to save us! I cannot tell what things are real and what are not!

BLIND MAN Oh, but it is not myself that is dark at all, but them—blind and drunk with the brave sight of their own eyes. For why would they care that the winds is cold and the beds is hard and the sewers do be stinking and steaming under the stone sets of the streets, when they can see a bit of a rag floating in the wild wind, and they dancing their bloody Ceilidhes[202] over the lip of Hell! Oh, I have my own way of seeing surely. It takes a dark man to see the will-o'-the-wisps and the ghosts of the dead and the half dead and them that will never die while they can find lazy, idle hearts ready to keep their venom warm.

SPEAKER [*up*] Out of the depths I have cried to Thee, O Lord: Lord, hear my voice![203]

BLIND MAN In every dusty corner lurks the living word of some dead poet, and it waiting for to trap and to snare them. This is no City of the Living: but of the Dark and the Dead!

SPEAKER I am mad—mad—mad! Sally!

[*During his speech the stage darkens until both figures are blotted out and the* SPEAKER *is left groping in the dark.*]

SARAH'S VOICE Robert! Robert!

SPEAKER What was that?

SARAH'S VOICE [*singing*]

> She stretched forth her arms,
> Her mantle she flung to the wind,
> And swam o'er Loch Leane
> Her outlawed lover to find . . . [204]

SPEAKER Sally! Sally! Where are you?

202. "Ceilidhes" A traditional Irish dancing and musical session.
203. "Out of the depths . . . hear my voice." Psalm 130 in the King James Version of the Bible, 129 in the Catholic Vulgate.
204. "She stretched forth . . . lover to find." See note 10.

SARAH'S VOICE Why don't you come to me, Robert? I have been waiting for you so long.

SPEAKER I have been searching for you so long.

SARAH'S VOICE I thought you had forgotten me.

SPEAKER Forgotten you! Forgotten you, Sally! Is that your hand, dear? *A chuisle me chroí*[205]—'Tis you shall have a silver throne—Her sunny mouth dimples with hope and joy: her dewy eyes are full of pity. It is you, Sally—Deirdre is mine: she is my Queen, and no man now can rob me!

[*The lights go up. He is in the dingy room of a tenement house. The plaster is peeling off the walls. On a bed in the corner a young man with the face of JOE is lying with an expression of serene contentment upon his pale, drawn features. Two men—the OLDER and the YOUNGER MAN—are playing cards at a table opposite, upon which stands a bottle with a candle perched rakishly in the neck. The SPEAKER himself is affectionately clasping the arm of the old FLOWER WOMAN. When he sees her he bursts into hysterical laughter.*]

WOMAN Ah, me lovely gentleman, is it me yer calling?

SPEAKER Well done! Well done! The joke is on me! Well done!

WOMAN The Lord love ye, an' how's the poor head?

SPEAKER Robert Emmet knows when the joke is on him! Kiss me, lovely Sarah Curran!

WOMAN [*archly*] Ah, go on owa that! D'jever hear the like!

OLDER MAN [*looking up from his game*] Drunk.

YOUNGER MAN Aw, disgustin'.

WOMAN Sit down now. Ah, go along with ye! Sit down now there, an' take no heed a them ignerant yucks . . . an' I'll get ye a small drop.

SPEAKER My lovely Sarah Curran! Sweet Sally!

WOMAN [*aside to the OLDER MAN*] Ye bloody rip! I'll twist the tongue of ye, that's what I will.

SPEAKER Her sunny mouth dimples with hope and joy.

YOUNGER MAN Ho, yes, you'll do the hell of a lot, ma . . . in me eye!

WOMAN Don't heed them. Don't heed them at all mister. He's no son of mine that has ne'er a soft word in his heart

---

205. *"A chuisle me chroí"* My heart's beloved.

for th' old mudher that reared him in sickness and in sorra te be a heart-scaldin' affliction an' a theef a honest names.

OLDER MAN Now ye can say what ye like, but there's a Man! There's a Man! Drunk, an' it's hours after closin'! Drunk, an' in th' old green coat! [*Singing.*] Oh, wrap the green flag round me, boys.

SPEAKER [*joins in*] Ta-ra-ra-ra-ra-ra, Ra! Ra!

WOMAN Sure, he's not drunk are ye, gentleman, an' if he was itself it's none a your concern. [*To* SPEAKER.] Isn't that right, son?

OLDER MAN And why the hell shouldn't he be drunk? Tell me that. We're a Free State,[206] aren't we? Keep open the pubs. That's my motto. What man says we're not a Free State?

YOUNGER MAN I say it, ye drunken bastard!

OLDER MAN Drunken bastard . . . hell! I declare to God I'm sober'n you are, me bold, water-drinkin' Diehard.[207] God knows I'm cold an odd time, but sure a true Patriot is always drunk.

YOUNGER MAN Have you no love for Ireland?

SPEAKER God save Ireland!

OLDER MAN Ho yes—'The Republic still lives'. Aw— go te hell!

YOUNGER MAN I've been to hell all right, never fear. I went down into hell shouting 'Up the living Republic', and I came up out of hell still shouting 'Up the living Republic'. Do you hear me? Up the Republic!

SPEAKER Up the Priory!

OLDER MAN Oh, I hear you well enough. But you'll not convince me for all your bridge blasting. Looka here, I stand for the status q-oh, and I'll not be intimidated by the gun.

WOMAN [*handing the* SPEAKER *a precious black bottle*][208] Here, have another sup and never heed that old chat of them!

SPEAKER A health, Sarah Curran! A toast to the woman with brave sons!

206. "Free State" The older man accepts the partition of Ireland and its dominion status.
207. "Diehard" Term for those, like the Younger Man, who refuse to accept the 1921 Free State compromise, insisting on the unification of the whole island in an Irish Republic.
208. "black bottle" Poteen, Ireland's illegally distilled whiskey.

WOMAN Aw God . . . If I was young again!

YOUNGER MAN And who needs to convince you?

OLDER MAN Oh, you needn't think . . .

YOUNGER MAN Every day and every night while you were lying on your back snoring, wasn't I out in the streets shouting 'Up the living Republic'?

OLDER MAN Ah, don't we remember that too well.

SPEAKER Up the living Departed!

YOUNGER MAN Every morning and every night while you were sitting in the old snug, wasn't I out on the hills shouting 'Up the living Republic'?

SPEAKER Up the pole![209]

OLDER MAN Well?

YOUNGER MAN Every hour of the day that you spent filling your belly and gassing about your status q-oh, wasn't I crying 'Republic, Republic, Republic'?

OLDER MAN May God give ye a titther a sense some day.

SPEAKER Up the blood-red Phlegethon![210] Up Cocytus,[211] frozen lake of Hell!

OLDER MAN [turning for a moment] Aw, wouldn't that languidge disgust ye!

YOUNGER MAN So one day, me laddo, you woke up and found that the Republic did live after all. And would you like to know why?

OLDER MAN 'Tell me not in mournful numbers' . . .

YOUNGER MAN Just because I and my like had said so, and said so again, while you were too drunk and too lazy and too thick in the head to say anything at all. That's why. And then, with the rest of your kidney you hunched your shoulders, spat on your hands, and went back to your bed mumbling 'Up the Status q-oh'. So why the hell should I try to convince you?

SPEAKER A long speech. A strong speech. A toast to the son that speaks. A toast to the son that swills!

OLDER MAN Aw, that's all words. Nothing but bloody words. You can't change the world by words.

---

209. "Up the pole" Slang for "pregnant."

210. "*Phlegethon*" Boiling river of blood in the seventh circle of Dante's *Inferno* (Canto XII). In *Nine Rivers from Jordan,* Johnston describes it as "the place all the tyrants of history are scorched" (p. 70).

211. "*Cocytus*" Frozen lake on the floor of hell reserved for the worst sin in Dante's *Inferno* (Canto XXXII): treachery against family members, friends, or country.

YOUNGER MAN That's where you fool yourself! What other way can you change it? I tell you, we can make this country—this world—whatever we want it to be by saying so, and saying so again. I tell you it is the knowledge of this that is the genius and glory of the Gael!

SPEAKER Up the Primum Mobile![212] Up the graters of verdigreece. Up the Apes Pater Noster.[213]

JOE
> Cupping the crystal jewel-drops
> Girdling the singing of the silver stream . . .

[*He tries to scribble on the wall.*]

What was it? . . . the singing of the silver stream.

Damp acid-cups of meadowsweet . . .

SPEAKER Hello! There's the fellow I shot. Is he not gone yet? A toast to the son that dies!

WOMAN Ay . . . are ye lookin' for a bit of sport tonight?

SPEAKER I have had brave sport this night!

WOMAN Aw, mister . . . have a heart!

SPEAKER [*flaring up*] A heart!

[JOE *gives a short, contented laugh.*]

SPEAKER Do not do that. That is not the way to laugh.

YOUNGER MAN I tell you, what the likes of me are saying tonight, the likes of you will be saying tomorrow.

OLDER MAN Is that a fact? And may I be so bold as to in-quire what awtority you have for makin' that observation?

YOUNGER MAN Because we're the lads that make the world.

OLDER MAN You don't say!

SPEAKER [*passionately*] Then why have you made it as it is? Then will you stand before the Throne and justify your handiwork? Then will you answer to me for what I am?

YOUNGER MAN What are *you* talking about? You're only a bloody play-actor. If you were a man and not satisfied with the state of things, you'd alter them for yourself.

OLDER MAN [*holding out a bottle*] Aw, have a sup and dry up for God's sake!

[JOE *laughs again.*]

---

212. "*Primum Mobile*" Ninth and highest circle of heaven in Dante's *Paradiso*, just below the Empyrean.

213. "*Pater Noster*" Our Father, Latin name of God and of the most sacred prayer of the New Testament.

SPEAKER That blasphemous laugh! Do you not know you're going to die?

JOE [*laughing again*]

    Soft radiance of the shy new moon[214]
    Above the green gold cap of Kilmashogue
    Where . . .

SPEAKER Kilmashogue!

JOE

    Where of a summer's evening I have danced
    A saraband.

SPEAKER What of Kilmashogue? Look around you. Here! Don't you know me? I shot you.

JOE Well, please don't interrupt. [*He coughs.*]

WOMAN It's the cough that shivers ye, isn't it, son? Me poor lamb, will ye tell the gentleman . . . [*She goes as if to touch him.*]

JOE [*through his teeth*] Strumpet! Strumpet!

WOMAN Blast ye! ye'd use that word t'yer own mudher, would ye! God, I'll throttle ye with me own two hands for the dirty scut ye are!

SPEAKER Go back!

YOUNGER MAN [*seizing her from behind and flinging her away*] Away to hell, ye old trollop!

OLDER MAN Ah, leave her alone.

WOMAN Awlright, awlright! Yer all agin me. But it won't be th' cough will have th' stiffenin' of him not if I lay me hands on his dirty puss before he's gone. When I get a holt a ye I'll leave me mark on ye never fear.

YOUNGER MAN Aw, shut yer mouth, ma!

JOE I'd like to do it all again . . . That's right . . . Again . . . It's good . . . to feel the wind . . . in your hair . . .
[*He laughs weakly.*]

SPEAKER Don't! Don't do that I tell you!

JOE

    Stench of the nut-brown clay
    Piled high around the headstones and the yews,
    My fingers clotted with the crusted clay,
    My heart is singing . . . in the skies . . .

[*He coughs again. The BLIND FIDDLER enters slowly through the door.*]

214. "Soft radiance of the shy new moon . . . " See Introduction, pp. 41–42.

114

OLDER MAN You know, some of that stuff is very hard to follow. I'd sooner have the old stuff any day.

> 'Oh I met with Napper Tandy
> An' he took me by the hand.'[215]

SPEAKER Sssssh!

YOUNGER MAN What do you want here?

BLIND MAN Wouldn't I have a right to pay my respects to one, and he passin' into the ranks of the Government? Isn't it a comely thing for me to be hopin' that he'll remember a poor old dark man an' he sittin' in the seats of the mighty in his kingdom out beyond?

JOE [*very soft*] Well . . . so long, lads. It was . . . a grand life . . . so long, lad . . . that plugged me . . So long . . . [*He dies.*]

WOMAN Burn ye! Burn ye!

BLIND MAN Be silent now, and a new shadow after being born! Do you not know, woman, that this land belongs not to them that are on it, but to them that are under it.

YOUNGER MAN He's gone. Stiffening already, poor chap. Hats off, lads.

SPEAKER Gone! And I am only a play-actor—unless I dare to contradict the dead! Must I do that?[216]

BLIND MAN Let them build their capitols on Leinster Lawn.[217] Let them march their green battalions out by the Park Gate. Out by Glasnevin[218] there's a rattle of bones and a bit of a laugh where the presidents and senators of Ireland are dancing hand in hand, with no one to see them but meself an' I with the stick an' the fiddle under me arm.

OLDER MAN Well . . . a wake's a wake, anyhow. So pass over the bottle and give us a tune on the ole instrument.

BLIND MAN [*tuning up*] It's many's the year an' I fiddled at a wake.

WOMAN One son with th' divil in hell, an' two more with th' divils on earth. [*She spits.*] God forgive me for weanin' a brood a sorry scuts!

---

215. "Oh I met with Napper Tandy . . . by the hand." From the street ballad "Wearing of the Green," commemorating the 1798 Rebellion of the United Irishmen and its Dublin leader, Napper Tandy.

216. "Gone! And I am only a play-actor. . . . Must I do that!" See Introduction, p. 41–42.

217. "Leinster Lawn" The grounds of Leinster House on Kildare Street in central Dublin, seat of the Irish *Oireachtas* or Parliament.

218. "Glasnevin" Prospect Cemetery in Glasnevin, suburb of north Dublin. See note 135.

[*The* SPEAKER *is seated silently at the foot of the bed, staring at the body with his back to the audience. There is a knock at the door.*]

WOMAN Wha's that?

[*The* YOUNGER MAN *goes to the door, pauses, and flings it open. On the threshold stands* MAEVE.]

MAEVE My mammy thez . . .

WOMAN Ah love, is it yerself?

MAEVE My mammy thez I'm to play the accompaniment of 'The Thruggle Ith Over'.

WOMAN Come on in, duckie. God love ye an' welcome. The ole pianner's waiting for ye, love.

MAEVE Yeth pleathe. My mammy . . .

[*She comes in and, catching sight of the* SPEAKER, *she points, and bursts into tears.*]

WOMAN There, there! What's the matter, lamb? Ah God help her! What ails ye at all?

MAEVE [*gulping*] Thlipperth . . .

WOMAN There, there now . . .

OLDER MAN Aw, will ye dry up?

WOMAN [*with an impatient flap of the hand*] There's the pianner, so do what yer mammy says before I slaughter ye.

BLIND MAN Play on now, young one. And when you've played, 'tis meself will fiddle for the shadows and they dancing at the wake.

MAEVE [*sniffling*] My mammy thez . . .

[MAEVE *sits at an old cracked piano, upon which presently she commences to thump out carefully 'The Struggle Is Over'.*]

WOMAN There now. Ah God, hasn't she the gorgus touch on th' ole instrument!

[*Another knock at the door. The* YOUNGER MAN *opens it. The* MINISTER FOR ARTS AND CRAFTS *is on the threshold in top hat, frock coat, and carrying one of those hemispherical glass cases full of white flowers.*]

MINISTER Deep concern—Government grieved to learn —struck down in prime—Requiem Mass—life for Erin—send a gunboat—bitter loss—token of our regard. [*He presents the case.*]

WOMAN [*very unctuous*] Ah, aren't ye the kind-hearted Government, and isn't them th' gorgus flowers. God will reward ye, sir; He will indeed at the next election, for th' blessed pity ye've shown to a poor woman in her sorra.

[*Another knock at the door. The* YOUNGER MAN *opens it.*
LADY TRIMMER, *dressed in widow's weeds, enters.*]
LADY TRIMMER So sad! So sad indeed! I can't simply
say how sad it is. Quite a poet, too, I hear. Can any of his
books be purchased?
WOMAN At Hodges an' Figgis[219] ma'am. Be sure ye get
the name right. Come in, come in!
[*Before the* YOUNGER MAN *has the door properly closed
there comes another knock. He abandons it, leaving it open. The*
STATUE OF GRATTAN *is on the threshold.*]
GRATTAN A word-spinner dying gracefully, with a cliché
on his lips. The symbol of Ireland's genius. Never mind. He
passed on magnificently. He knew how to do that.
WOMAN [*her head quite turned*] An' he was me favrit', too
lady . . . never a bitter word . . . never a hard glance. Sure, it's
them we love th' best is took th' first, God help us. Ullagone!
Ullagone! Ochone-a-ree!
[*Enter the* GENERAL *with crape upon his arm.*]
GENERAL . . . a grand song called 'Home to Our Mountains'. No. 17 bus passes the door or a bus to Ballyboden,[220]
whenever the road's not up. But of course if you don't want me
to sing, I won't force myself on you. Won't I?
WOMAN

        Low lie your heads this day
        My sons! My sons!
        The strong in their pride go by me
        Saying, 'Where are thy sons?'[221]

[O'COONEY, O'MOONEY, *and* O'ROONEY *enter, all
in black gloves and top hats.*]
ALL THREE Who's a twister? I'm a twister? You're a
twister? He's taken a header into the Land of Youth. Anyhow,
he was a damn sight better man than some I could name, and
there's no blottin' it out.
LADY TRIMMER So yellow-haired Donough is dead![222]
Dear, dear!
[*A few more stray figures crush in, chattering and pressing forward in file before the body.*]

219. "Hodges an' Figgis" Bookstore on Grafton Street in 1920s.
220. "Ballyboden" Suburb south of Rathfarnham.
221. "Low lie your heads . . . thy sons?" "The Little Lamentation," Todhunter.
222. "yellow-haired Donough is dead" Yeats's *Cathleen ni Houlihan*, p. 82.

WOMAN
> Gall to our heart! Oh, gall to our heart!
> Ullagone! Ochone-a-ree!
> A lost dream to us now in our home!

MAEVE [*stopping her playing*] Will that do, Daddy?

BLIND MAN [*mounting upon a chair*] The shadows are gathering, gathering. They're coming to dance at a wake. An' I playin' for them on the gut box. Are yez ready all?

[*He tunes up. The lights in front have dimmed, leaving a great sheet of brightness flooding from the sides upon the back-cloth. The walls of the room seem to fade apart while the crowd draws aside and seats itself upon the floor and upon all sides of the stage. The SPEAKER has vanished.*]

THE VOICES OF THE CROWD The Shadows are gathering, gathering: he says they must dance at a wake. Seats for the Shadows the gathering Shadows . . . The Shadows that dance at a wake.

[*The BLIND MAN commences to fiddle a jig in the whole-tone scale.*]

THE VOICES Overture started
> Seats for the Shadows
> Gathering, gathering
> Dance at a wake
> Loosen his collar
> Basin of water
> Dance Shadows
> Ooooooh!

[*Upon the back-cloth two great SHADOWS appear gesturing and posturing in time with the music.*]

THE FIRST SHADOW [*stopping his dance and striking an attitude*]
> Come clear of the nets of wrong and right;
> Laugh, heart, again in the grey twilight,
> Sigh, heart, again in the dew of the morn.
> Your Mother Eire is always young . . .[223]

[*Hand clapping. The SECOND SHADOW jostles the FIRST aside and points one long arm vaguely in the direction of the FLOWER WOMAN.*]

---

223. "Come clear of the nets . . . is always young . . . " Slight misquotation of Yeats's poem "Into the Twilight," p. 65.

THE SECOND SHADOW Stone traps of dead builders. Warrens of weasel rats.[224] How serene does she now arise! Queen among the Pleiades, in the penultimate antelucan hour: shod in sandals of bright gold: coifed with a veil of gossamer.[225]

[*Applause. Amidst shrieks of laughter the* FLOWER WOMAN *rises, curtsies and dances hilariously once round the foreground. Two more* SHADOWS *have elbowed the first pair aside and are now dancing to the music.*]

THE VOICES Dance! Dance!
Speak, Shadows, speak!

THE THIRD SHADOW It is difficult not to be unjust to what one loves. Is not He who made misery wiser than thou?[226]

[*Applause, mingled with some booing. The* THIRD SHADOW *throws up its arms and flees.*]

THE FOURTH SHADOW Every dream is a prophecy: every jest an earnest in the womb of time.[227]

[*Shouts of laughter and applause. The* SHADOWS *change into a tumbling mass of blackness.*]

THE VOICES Dance! Dance!
Speak, Shadows, speak!

A VOICE There are no Shadows left to speak.

BLIND MAN Speak, great Shadow! Shadow of Ireland's Heart.

VOICES [*whispering*] We see him. He is here.

[*The shadow of the* SPEAKER *precedes him as he comes slowly in from the back.*]

BLIND MAN Speak, shadow of Robert Emmet.

SPEAKER I know whom you are calling. I am ready.

BLIND MAN The eyes of the people are fixed on your face.

VOICES Justify! Justify! Shadow of the Speaker, speak!

VOICES Sssh!

SPEAKER The souls in the seven circles of Purgatory cry out, Deliver us O Lord from the mouth of the Lion that Hell

---

224. "Stone traps..weasel rats!" Slight misquotation from Joyce's "Proteus" in *Ulysses* 3, line 289.

225. "How serene does she . . . veil of gossamer." Slight misquotation from "Oxen of the Sun," *Ulysses* 14, lines 1102–4.

226. "Is not He . . . wiser than thou?" Oscar Wilde, *De Profundis*, p. 83.

227. "Every dream is a prophecy . . . womb of time." Lines of Father Keegan in Shaw's *John Bull's Other Island*, 2:1021.

may not swallow us up.[228] The Word Made Flesh[229] shall break the chains that bind me. Three armies may be robbed of their leader—no wretch can be robbed of his will.

Yes, there is darkness now, but I can create light.[230] I can separate the waters of the deep,[231] and a new world will be born out of the void. A challenge, Norns![232] A gage flung down before you! Justify! Justify!

VOICES Justify! Justify!

[*The SPEAKER continues to address the audience.*]

SPEAKER [*continues*] Race of men with dogs' heads! Panniers filled with tripes and guts![233] Thelemites![234] Cenobites![235] Flimflams[236] of the law! Away! while Niobe[237] still weeps over her dead children. I have heard the angels chanting the Beatitudes to the souls in Malebolge,[238] and I have done with you.

I do not fear to approach the Omnipotent Judge to answer for the conduct of my short life and am I to stand appalled here before this mere remnant of mortality? I do not imagine that Your Lordships will give credit to what I utter. I have no hopes that I can anchor my character in the breast of this court. I only

228. "The souls in the seven circles of Purgatory. . . . not swallow us up." For his harrowing of hell/Dublin, the Speaker borrows from a number of western mythologies, beginning here with Dante's *Purgatorio* where the suffering souls sit on seven ledges. The leopard, she-wolf, and lion block Dante's path, but in this context, only the lion, allegorical representation of pride, poses a threat. Since this speech begins the Speaker's heretical challenge, the lion here may refer as well to William Blake's "Proverbs of Hell" in *The Marriage of Heaven and Hell* (Pl.8, line 24): "The wrath of the lion is the wisdom of God."

229. "Word Made Flesh" Jesus Christ (John 1:14).

230. "I can create light." Reference to the description of Yahweh's creation of the world in Gen. 1:3.

231. "I can separate the waters of the deep." Reference to Moses parting the waters of the Red Sea (Exod. 14:21–22).

232. "Norns" Three Norse goddesses of fate.

233. "Race of men . . . tripes and guts!" Insults adapted from inscriptions on the Great Gate of the Abbey of Thélème. Rabelais, *Gargantua and Pantagruel*, pp. 160–83.

234. "Thelemites" Symbol of religious decadence in *Gargantua and Pantagruel*, specifically the religious of the Abbey of Thélème, whose motto was: "Do what thou wilt."

235. "Cenobites" The religious who live together in communities as opposed to those who choose to live alone as anchorites.

236. "Flimflams" Deceptions.

237. "Niobe" A figure in Greek myth whose children were killed by Artemis and Apollo after she boasted of their superiority to Leto. Zeus changed her into a mountain whose streams are her tears.

238. "I have heard the angels . . . souls in Malebolge." Dante's eighth circle of Hell (canto XVIII), where the souls convicted of malicious fraud are condemned to suffer eternally, and would therefore never hear angels chanting Christ's Beatitudes.

wish Your Lordships may suffer it to float down your memories until it has found some more hospitable harbour to shelter it.[239]

[*Voices, shuffling, applause.*]

SPEAKER [*continues*] For now is the axe put to the root of the tree. My fan is in my hand, and I will burn the chaff with unquenchable fire.[240]

VOICES Up Emmet!

Up Rathfarnham!

Up the Up that won't be Down!

[*He draws his sword and turns upon them all. During the following commination the* VOICES *give the responses in unison and the* FIGURES *in turn fling up their arms and take flight before him. The light fades, gradually blotting out all vestiges of the room.*]

SPEAKER Cursed[241] be he who values the life above the dream.

VOICES Amen.

SPEAKER Cursed be he who builds but does not destroy.

VOICES Amen.

SPEAKER Cursed be he who honours the wisdom of the wise.

VOICES Amen.

SPEAKER Cursed be the ear that heeds the prayer of the dead.

VOICES Amen.

SPEAKER Cursed be the eye that sees the heart of a foe.

VOICES Amen.

SPEAKER Cursed be prayers that plough not, praises that reap not, joys that laugh not, sorrows that weep not.

VOICES [*dying away*] Amen. Amen. Ah—men.

[*The last of the* FIGURES *fling up their arms and vanish. As the* SPEAKER *comes down stage they come creeping back again, crouching in the darkness and watching him with many eyes. It is dark.*]

239. "I do not fear to approach . . . harbour to shelter it." The historical Emmet's dock speech. Since his speech was reconstructed later by trial witnesses, no one is certain of the exact words, but these have become the canonical version.

240. "For now is the axe . . . burn the chaff with unquenchable fire." This quotation (Luke 3:9, 17) is part of the Anglican Commination Service for Ash Wednesday, Johnston's favorite liturgy.

241. "Cursed" The following litany of six curses is the Speaker's Credo of the Invincibles, inspired by Blake's "Damn braces, bless relaxes" in "Proverbs of Hell," Pl. 9.

SPEAKER I will take this earth in both my hands and batter it into the semblance of my heart's desire![242] See, there by the trees is reared the gable of the house where sleeps my dear one. Under my feet the grass is growing, soft and subtle, in the evening dew. The cool, clean wind is blowing down from Killakee,[243] kissing my hair and dancing with the flowers that fill the garden all around me. And Sarah . . . Sarah Curran . . . you are there . . . waiting for Robert Emmet.

I know this garden well for I have called it into being with the Credo of the Invincibles:[244] I believe in the might of Creation, the majesty of the Will, the resurrection of the Word, and Birth Everlasting.

[*He flings aside his sword and looks around him in triumph. It is very dark, so dark that for all we know perhaps it may be the garden of the first scene. Perhaps those may be the trees and the mountains beyond the Priory. For a moment we hear the tramp of feet and the distant sound of the Shan Van Vocht. His voice falters and he staggers wearily.*]

SPEAKER My ministry is now ended. Shall we sit down together for a while? Here on the hillside . . . where we can look down over the city, and watch the lights twinkle and wink to each other . . . Our city . . . our wilful, wicked old city . . .

[*The gauze curtains close slowly behind him.*]

I think . . . I would like to sleep . . . What? . . . On your shoulder? . . . Ah, I was so right to go on!

[*His head sinks drowsily and his eyes stare out into the auditorium. He is lying just where the* DOCTOR *left him some time ago.*]

Strumpet city in the sunset[245]

Suckling the bastard brats of Scots, of Englishry, of Huguenot.

Brave sons breaking from the womb, wild sons fleeing from their Mother.

Wilful city of savage dreamers,

---

242. "I will take this earth . . . my heart's desire." Paraphrased from stanza 73 of Fitzgerald's *Rubaiyat of Omar Khayyam*. See note 70 of Introduction.

243. "Killakee" Literally, the Blind Man's wood; part of the Dublin Mountains, south of the city.

244. "Invincibles" Irish revolutionaries who formed the secret assassination club that killed the British Chief Secretary Lord Frederick Cavendish and his under-secretary in Phoenix Park, 1882.

245. "Strumpet City in the sunset" Adapted from Shaw's *Saint Joan*, 6:117: "Strumpet wind in the Sunset on the Loire."

So old, so sick with memories!
Old Mother
Some they say are damned,
But you, I know, will walk the streets of Paradise
Head high, and unashamed.
[*His eyes close. He speaks very softly.*]
There now. Let my epitaph be written.
[*There is silence for a moment and then the* DOCTOR *speaks off.*]
DOCTOR . . . do, fine.[246]
[*He appears bearing a large and gaudy rug. He looks towards the audience, places one finger to his lips, and makes a sign for the front curtains to be drawn. When last we see him he is covering the unconscious* SPEAKER *with his rug. That is the end of this play.*]

BLOOMSBURY, 1926–DALKEY, 1976.

246. " . . . do, fine." See Introduction, p. 45.

A NOTE ON WHAT HAPPENED

(The following note was originally published as program notes
for the 1935 production of the play in the United States.)

Walking back from Sorrento with Mr Yeats he gave me
what was probably the most incisive criticism this play has received. 'I liked your play,' he said, 'but it has one or two faults.
The first is, the scenes are too long.' He was silent for a time,
while we both gazed with some signs of embarrassment at a
cargo boat rounding Dalkey Island. 'Then', he added finally
and after considerable thought, 'there are too many scenes.'

Needless to say I was grateful for this opinion.

To say that the scenes are too long and that there are too
many of them goes right to the root of the matter. Why do it at
all? And if it does mean anything, isn't it better left unsaid?

A distinguished member of the audience who sat through
most of the performance with his eyes closed remarked very
aptly as he took himself home, 'I suppose people must have
nightmares, but why inflict them on us?' I am afraid I can sup-
ply very little in the way of an answer. Perhaps nightmares—or
dreams, if you're that kind—don't really mean very much, and
probably a good many of them would be better left unremem-
bered. Ireland is spiritually in a poor condition at the moment
and I don't know that homeopathic treatment is the best for her
complaint. A young lady having seen the play said of it that it
made her blush. Not because of its vulgarity—ordinary vulgarity was a commonplace on the stage. But this was different.
She had blushed for me—that such thoughts should ever have
entered my head.

This play, if plays must be about something, is about what
Dublin has made a good many of us feel. And if it is a very
wrong and vulgar feeling that could only have been experienced by people with nasty minds, we aren't worth bothering

about anyway. But it is no good saying that it isn't true, because we happen to know that it is.

I was warned during rehearsals by various friends that the play would be denounced as anti-National, or as Republican propaganda, or as a personal reflection on so-and-so—opinions which were given with the best of good will but whose only common denominator was that the play would be denounced. In this they were right, but only in their conclusions. For as it turned out when the production was complete the assault came from a most unexpected quarter. It was well patronised by *l'ancien regime* and was stoutly defended in the press and elsewhere by more than one physical force Intransigentist. But exception was taken to the play on the ground that it was blasphemous.

It appeared that the language of the Holy Writ was used in obscene circumstances—ranted and raved by a mad actor to the accompaniment of a chorus of curses and swearwords—that the scene in which some of these lines were spoken was a brothel—and that the final Commination was a ribald parody of Jesus driving the money-changers from the Temple.

I need hardly say that I was not prepared for this, although I was ready to be philosophic about the charge that I was trying to write a silly lampoon of living persons. But now that I come to think of it, I have noticed before that the words of Holy Writ when used in circumstances in which they are liable to be taken seriously sometimes incur the suspicion of being either insanity or blasphemy.

I can quite appreciate the point of view which holds that the ethics of religion are solely a matter for the pulpit and have no place upon the stage.

But granted that we have persuaded all those members of the audience to leave the theatre if they are the kind who experience a shock on discovering that their own theological ideas have a human and a dramatic meaning as well as a symbolic one; how then, are we to express on the stage the idea of the triumph of the Word over environment—the dogma of the Resurrection? It seems to me that the most straightforward way —especially in a play where all other ideas are conveyed by the thematic method—is to call up the desired association of ideas by suggesting the words of the Liturgy.

Whether or not I have succeeded in doing this myself is

another matter, but the fact that I appear to have suggested to the minds of some of my critics the picture of the expulsion of the money-changers from the Temple—an analogy which was not before my own mind—would indicate that I have not entirely failed.

And lest it should be thought that criticisms of this kind are not of much consequence these days, I should add that nearly every night indignant women walked out during the last act, and strong representations were made to the authorities to have a blasphemy prosecution set on foot. Needless to say the authorities had no time to waste on such small fry as the little Gate Theatre or myself, but the threat had high ramifications and results that it would be amusing but totally wrong of me to disclose.

*   *   *   *

I think that it must be a result of the long predominance of narrative drama to the exclusion of all else that people get so worried when one cannot tell them what a play is about. Yet the dithyrambic outbursts from which both western and eastern theatrical conventions have developed had nothing to do with a plot. It would be difficult to interpret the religious ecstacy of a mediaeval miracle play or the intricacies of a No Play of Japan for inclusion in French's 'Guide to Selecting Plays'.

It seems to me that the real play must be regarded as what goes on in the mind of the audience. What, therefore, a play is about depends entirely on who is listening to it.

Anybody who has done any acting will know that a performance to an audience is quite a different affair from the most complete Dress Rehearsal—as different as War is from Salisbury Plain. And furthermore, a good play—that is to say, a play which is succeeding in registering its effect whether we personally approve of it or not—is a different play from night to night according as the reflex of the House varies.

And these ideas and emotions can be stimulated without the assistance of a narrative plot at all, whether melodically as in music, by direct statement as in continental Expressionism, or by simple association of ideas. Strindberg in some of his later work provides one of the best modern examples of the fact that dramatic experience is not dependent on physical actuality and is in fact hampered by it. In the 'Spook Sonata' there is for example, the wretched wife who sits all day in a

127

dark cupboard from which she cries like a parrot, 'Pretty Polly! Pretty Polly!' This genius with which he conveys an attitude of mind in terms of a fantastic physical reality has, on me at any rate, a most real and horrifying effect, but the intention of the author is completely defeated if the audience insists on regarding the picture as one of narrative fact.

The melodic method has been greatly developed since the War by the Russians, principally in the Constructivist Theatre of Meierhold and in the Moscow Jewish Art Theatre, where an attempt is made to stimulate the desired attitude of mind by means of acrobatics and dancing and the elimination of all unnecessary detail in the way of stage decor or scenery. The development of electric lighting has of course opened up limitless possibilities in all those directions.

Toller and Kaiser taking the dangerous course of direct statement have so simplified the stage by throwing out unnecessary lumber that nothing will convince a British audience, schooled to the loud technical camouflage of Mr St. John Irvine, that they are really saying anything at all. They have however discredited their school to some extent in the eyes of non-industrial audiences by a complete absence of humour and by the Frankenstein complex that seems to have dominated the stage of Central Europe ever since the War.

In English-speaking countries on the other hand, the tradition of Pinero, Barker and Shaw, culminating in the 'Problem Play', is still well entrenched in the path of any further development of the theatre. We have the Play that leaves you with a Thought. What would I do if I met an Escaped Convict? How would I like it if Father married a Prostitute? Is War Right? I need hardly say that as a natural consequence nobody can go to an ostensibly serious play without feeling that he must concentrate upon what it is all About.

But surely this is all wrong, just as it would be in the case of music! All that is needed to enjoy and appreciate a work such as e.e. cummings' 'Him' is a simple faith, a little human experience, and a receptive state of mind attained by a process the reverse of concentration. This being the normal condition of my own mind I need hardly say that I find little difficulty in preferring Strindberg's 'Dream Play' to 'Emperor and Galillean'.

*   *   *   *

'The Old Lady says "No"!' is not an expressionist play [in the German tradition] and ought never to have been mistaken for one. I have attempted to evolve a thematic method based on simple association of ideas, a process which has as many disadvantages as the opposite. For it presupposes at the start a set of recognisable figments in the minds of the audience—figments which from their very nature are bound to be somewhat local. In consequence of this, the play to be intelligible to a non-Irish audience requires to some extent to be translated.

The theme of the Romantic temperament seeking for an environment in which to express himself is a universal one, but everybody cannot be expected to know about Robert Emmet. When an old lady appears upon the stage and maunders about her four beautiful green fields, it is too much to expect of a London audience that it will recognise the traditional figure of romantic Nationalism for whom Mangan and Pearse sighed. It is only in the Free State that the O'Donovan Rossa speech and Committee Room 15 (where Parnell was betrayed) can be relied upon to call up any recollections without the aid of a footnote.

Yet the search for the Land of Heart's Desire is as old and as universal as the Holy Grail. The tale might also be the tale of such diverse figures as Juan Ponce de Leon, of the great Danton, of Abelard, of John Brown of Harper's Ferry and even of poor William Blake. Every land has had its store of Emmets, preaching their burning messages to the accompaniment of farmyard noises, and Ireland has more than her share.

It was Plato who first told us that if we don't like our environment it is up to us to alter it for ourselves, and the vigorous philosophy of Nietzsche's Man-Gott and the biology of Buffon and Lamarck are in somewhat the same line of business. If the Emmets in particular or if intransigent Irish Republicanism in general are to be taken as having made any contribution to the world of applied philosophy I feel that it is this characteristic attitude of mind. 'The Republic still lives' is not the expression of a pious hope, but is in itself a creative act, as England knows to her cost.

I understand that there is a correct psychological explanation of all this. Ned Stephens, for instance, tells me that the play represents the breaking down of something called a 'synthetic personality' by contact with reality and the creation of a new one in its stead. I am much too scared of Freud, Adler and McDougall ever to have attempted any such thing, but I feel that if a play is true to experience in its emotional aspect it may well have a sound psychological meaning thrown in as well. As a small boy I used to make pictures for myself with a box of blocks. When the work was completed I used to find that by turning the whole over you found another finished picture constructed on the other side.

But I should add that all this is not intended to be by way of explanation. All that I do wish to do is to answer the objection levelled at much of the post-war spirit both in art and in letters; that it is insincere, intentionally obscure and that it lacks fundamentality. Lucidity seems to me to be the *sine qua non* of any effort of this kind. It has not been my desire to detract attention from my lack of craftsmanship by muddling people's minds. Neither have I any desire that the play should be unjustly enhanced by the 'false glitter of quotations', as one critic very threateningly put it. The method is thematic and a motif in the realm of thought is carried best by a name or a quotation.

Some years ago I used to have to play a game where some large, blindfold person, groping round with a cushion, would sit on my knee and tell me to 'Make a noise like a camel'. Well in this play when I want to make a noise like the Old Ireland, I do it in what seems to me to be the easiest way—by means of a potted anthology of the 'Erin a tear and a smile' school that preceded Geoffrey Phibbs. The play with which the first part opens, and which crops up again at intervals, is almost entirely composed of well-known lines from Mangan, Moore, Callinan, Blacker, Griffin, Ferguson, Kickham, Todhunter and a dozen more. The voices of the Shadows are the easily recognisable words of some of Dublin's greatest contributors to the World's knowledge of itself. The long speech with which the play concludes contains suggestions from Emmet's speech from the dock, the resurrection thesis of the Litany, and the magnificent, though sadly neglected, Commination Service of the Anglican Church.

I have already drawn attention to the Old Woman's lines. For the rest I have not consciously or wilfully bowdlerised anybody, except one line of Blake's which I freely admit I am not entitled to, but which is too apt to be surrendered. You may have it if you can find it!

But whatever may be said of the play, there can be no two opinions as to the merits of Hilton Edward's production. It was staged on a space roughly 16 feet by 12 feet—an incredible feat, when it is remembered that at several points there are mass movements of crowds that have to be carried out in a manner not dissimilar to a ballet, and that sets have to be changed while the action is proceeding.

The rhythmatic chanting of the Choruses was carried out to the throb of a drum, for which purpose a considerable portion of the dialogue had practically to be scored—the parts coming in one on top of the other as in instrumental music or a madrigal. It was an unusual and amusing sight at rehearsals to see the spoken lines being conducted from the front by the Producer. It would be invidious to refer to the players. The elan of Micheál MacLiammóir as the Speaker, the virtuosity of Meriel Moore in the difficult double role of Sarah Curran and the old woman, and the very trying work of the Chorus were the real cause of the play's success.

May I respectively thank them—not forgetting to include my friend Kate Curling for her help and for her contribution.

PERTISAU, 1929.

131

MUSIC FOR THE PLAY

Prepared by Art O'Murnaghan for first Gate Production

The Shan Van Vocht

1. Opening Chorus. Part I

Mike Magilligan's Daughter

2. Flower Woman. Part I

O, she's Mike Magilligan's daughter Mary Anne —— She has arms and legs up – on her like a man —— An' she doesn't paint nor powdher An' her figger is all her own For she's Mike Magilligan's daughter Ma–ry Anne ——

God Save Ireland

3. Speaker & Chorus. Part I

voices

God save Ireland, said the he – roes, God save Ireland, say we all; Whether on the scaffold high Or the battle – field we die, O, what mat – ter when for Er – in dear we fall!

Dies Irae

(Lacrymosa Dies Illa)

4. Chorus. Part I

arr. Art O'Murnaghan

1. La·cry·mo·sa di·es il·la /
   Qua re·sur·get ex fa·vil·la /
   Ju·di·can·dus ho·mo re·us.

2. Hu·ic er·go par·ce De·us /
   Pi·e Je·su Do·mi·ne /
   do·na e·is re·qui·em. A·men.

She Is Far from the Land

5. The General. Part II

The Struggle Is Over

6. Speaker & Blind Man. Part II

voices & violin

She Stretched Forth Her Arms

7. Sarah's voice. Part II

Lento

voice only

The Blind Man's Jig
[At the Gate]

8. Jig [whole–tone scale]. Part II

1929
Art O'Murnaghan
composition

violin

The Old Lady Says "No!"
was composed in 11/12 Bembo by
Marathon Typography Service, Inc.,
Durham, North Carolina, and printed
and bound by Braun-Brumfield, Inc.,
Ann Arbor, Michigan.